Lest We Forget

Stories originating from
*The Battle of Britain Memorial Flight
based at RAF Coningsby, Lincolnshire.*

Compiled and written by
Peter G. Rowland

Published by Lincolnshire Books

First published in Great Britain by Lincolnshire Books
© 1997 Peter G. Rowland

ISBN: 1-872375- 04-9

Designed, typeset and produced for the publishers
by Graphics Unit, Lincolnshire County Council

Printed by G.W. Belton Ltd., Gainsborough, Lincs

LINCOLNSHIRE BOOKS
Official publishers to Lincolnshire County Council
County Offices
Newland
Lincoln LN1 1YL

CONTENTS

Cover Photographs

1   Spitfire P7350 airborne. (Crown copyright/MoD) (See Chapter 1)

2   Five members of a Lancaster crew of 156 Squadron. May 1944. (Photograph courtesy of Peter Bond) (See Chapter 14)

3   Lancaster PA474 (Photograph courtesy of Sgt Keith Brenchley)

4   Hurricane PZ865 (Photograph courtesy of Sgt Keith Brenchley)

5   Spitfire P7350 (Photograph courtesy of Sgt Keith Brenchley)

INTRODUCTION
& acknowledgements

In what is probably a unique arrangement between the Royal Air Force and a Local Authority, the Battle of Britain Memorial Flight based at Coningsby in Lincolnshire is open to the public (for details see page 78). This collection of veteran aircraft is part of our national heritage. It includes the oldest Spitfire in airworthy condition, P7350 - the only aircraft to have fought in the actual battle; the Lancaster PA474, the only World War Two four-engined heavy bomber still flying in Europe, and the last Hurricane, PZ865, to come off the production line in 1944.

With the other aircraft in the Flight, they form a Display Team which takes part in airshows, squadron re-unions, and perform fly-pasts at many other events from April to October each year, in this country and indeed abroad. Earlier this year, Spitfire AB910 was dismantled and flown in an RAF Hercules transport to Nellis AFB, Nevada, where it was re-assembled and flown in the displays to mark the 50th anniversary of the founding of the United States Air Force.

Back in 1986, the Flight hangar was opened to the public provided they were in small groups with an official Guide in charge. This was where Lincolnshire County Council came in. Mindful of the County's links with the Royal Air Force from its earliest days, the Authority assumed responsibility for the recruitment, training and administration of the Guides. Some forty were appointed, the great majority being retired Service personnel, some with ground or air experience of the actual aircraft types.

The early days were experimental. The Guides occupied one room in the hangar buildings and the public were escorted some 300 yards from the nearest perimeter gateway - in all weathers! But it proved successful. Visitors came and seemed impressed with what they saw. Word got around.

Service personnel in the hangar, at first unused to being watched at work by civilians, gradually grew used to their new celebrity status. The apprehension of work interrupted by autograph hunters; of tools and spare parts disappearing as souvenirs, evaporated. Both the Service and County Council realised that the public appreciated the opportunity to see these superb aeroplanes on the ground at close quarters.

Expansion followed. The County Council set up a Visitors' Centre with static exhibitions and a shop in Service premises near the Dogdyke Road; a new entrance was created and a large car park established. A modest charge is levied, not with the intention of making a profit for what remains after running costs have been deducted is donated to the RAF Benevolent Fund. To date, some 209,000 people have visited the Flight - which is some measure of its value.

The genesis of this little book took place in 1990 as a result of several Guides listening to, and talking with visitors whom they had shown round the Flight. As one Guide said, "Those stories ought to be written down before they're forgotten and lost!"

And then it became, "If they're good enough to write down, then they're good enough for others to read!"

The stories and incidents are all genuine in that they actually happened. With one exception, the story-tellers are all known to me personally.

The stories are original in that - as far as I am aware - they have not been told in print before, except in a specialist or limited circulation journal. Where an episode involves another well-known story such as The Wooden Horse, or Operation Gisela, then this is always acknowledged and the reader referred to previously published work.

Finally, facts have been checked wherever possible. In some cases records are missing or were never kept, but pains have been taken to ensure authenticity. One story does not appear. When checking dates and places, it became clear that it could not have occurred. My guess is that two separate incidents had been run together in the teller's memory - not deliberately - but in a fifty-year old memory, such things do happen.

It's all taken a long time, but at last - here it is!

P.G.R.1997

ACKNOWLEDGEMENTS

My thanks are due to the Officer Commanding, Battle of Britain Memorial Flight, Squadron Leader Paul Day, AFC, RAF, for permission to use the Flight Crest and motto.

My thanks to all those who provided material: Squadron Leader Rick Groombridge RAF,; Warrant Officer Len Sutton, RAF; Guides Peter Bond; Mick Bridger; Bill Newman; Nelson Nix; Bob Panton, and Bill Rimmer.

To Norman Bradley; John Chatterton DFC; Jim Cole DFC; Douglas Eke, and Tom Wilson.

To Janet Brown for permission to print her original drawing.

To Stella Clarey for permission to print a cartoon by her late husband, Derrick Clarey.

To Mrs Madeleine Astbury for permission to print her letter.

My thanks are due to the following for permission to reproduce photographs: Sergeant Keith Brenchley RAF; Warrant Officer Len Sutton RAF; Mick Bridger; Peter Bond and the Crown Photographic Service, M.o D.

Finally to my good friend, John Richardson, whose comments and criticism have been invaluable.

THE ARMOURER'S STORY

Chapter 1

Throughout the land, 1990 has been commemorated as the 50th anniversary of the Battle of Britain. The Royal Air Force's Memorial Flight based at Coningsby has been much in evidence at airshows, fly-pasts, and squadron re-unions: the elderly have remembered the Few and the young have learnt. The Hurricanes and Spitfires of the Flight, superbly maintained, have provided tangible evidence; their Merlins evoked sighs of nostalgia from those to whom the sound was wartime reassurance.

This year, the Flight has had many visitors. Some were participants in the Battle; household names of the Forties, still honoured within the Service, they came to sit again in the aircraft that had once carried them into battle; to renew acquaintance and reminisce, and take in their stride the attentions of media, TV and film crews. Some were participants who never became household names.

One morning in early September, a Guide was conducting a party round the hangar. They were a mixed bunch of mums and dads with their offspring - a final visit before Term started; there was an American tourist and his wife; an Australian lad backpacking; an elderly man with a girl who could have been his grand-daughter.........

The Guide paused at each aircraft giving a resumé of its history and wartime function. They came,

Spitfire P7350 *as she appeared when visited by her Armourer in* 1990.

halfway down the hangar, to a gleaming Spitfire. "This, Ladies and Gentlemen, is our most historic fighter. When you see on your TV screens that fly-past over London in about a fortnight, you'll notice that it's lead by a single Spitfire. It will be this one; for she's the only aircraft that fought in the battle and is still flying today..........."

There was a buzz of appreciation from the party and a flurry of photographic activity. The elderly fellow was loud in his praise, "There she is ......now isn't she a beauty?" he enthused to the young lady. Then he edged forward and asked the Guide, "Can I touch her?"

The Guide smiled, and gently but firmly replied, "No, I'm afraid that's one thing you can't do."

The old fellow turned away, crestfallen and embarrassed at having been refused. Some sixth sense prompted the Guide to ask, "Any special reason why you asked?"

"Well, it's my aircraft, you see!"

"In what way?"

"I was her armourer. From when she arrived on the Squadron I took her over, saw her through the battle and on into '41. I was posted in......oh, the November, but I kept in touch with her."

The Guide turned to the rest of the party. "When we have someone who was so closely connected with the aircraft, I'm prepared to lend a hand.."

He explained the situation to an RAF Corporal who lifted up the rope. "Go ahead," said the Guide, and the old man stooped under. Then, straightening up, the armourer took a couple of paces and ran his hand gently over the tailplane and elevators. He patted the gunports, touched the wingtip and nodded approval.

"Hey!," called a transatlantic voice, "you just hold it right there!" The armourer posed, smiled and looked - not at the camera - but at his beloved aeroplane. Shutters clicked; lights flashed, the party suddenly found their voices.

"You must know a lot about this aircraft. Would you like to tell the rest of the party about her?" invited the Guide. The party fell silent again.

"Well," he began, "she was built in the Castle Bromwich factory in August 1940. She's a Mark II, and arrived on 266 squadron on the 2nd of September. When we got her, I remember........." He recalled her exploits; the men who flew her; the day she came back with bullet holes in her port wing; the trials of re-arming her, in the open, in a cold dawn with icy fingers............ten minutes later, he paused.

"You went right through the war?" enquired the Guide. He nodded.

"Then you must have serviced many aircraft. Why's this one so special?"

"Well, it's the serial number, you see. Sort of coincidence ...she's P7350." (He pointed to the number painted on the fuselage.) "Now I was courting a girl at the time and that was her phone number - seven three five oh."

"Did you marry the girl?" By now the entire party were listening intently....

"Oh, yes, I married her alright."

"And is your wife here with you today?"

Spitfire P7350 airborne.

"No. The aircraft's outlived her............" His voice trailed off.

No one knew what to say next. The party began to drift on in ones and twos. The Guide lifted the rope and helped the armourer back onto the walkway. "Thank you," he said, and then added in a burst, "you see, I had to see her today...........it's her birthday.!"

"How's that ?"

"Well, it's the fourth of September, isn't it? And it was on the fourth in 1940 that she flew into battle for the first time. Fifty years ago today....had to see her." A pause. and then, "I've had this day booked for over a year...........my niece brought me up from Ipswich.........good of her." And he patted the girl's arm.

"Yes," agreed the Guide. "We ought to move on. Now this aircraft is much later, built in 1945..............."

Under the black wing of the Lancaster they moved; into the corner. "Now let's move round to the rear of the aircraft. I want to show you the rear turret - the coldest and loneliest place in a night bomber." Round to the back of the Lancaster they filed. The Guide looked back. The armourer was still standing just behind Spitfire P7350; ramrod-straight, silent.

"We ought to join the others," his niece reminded him gently.

"Right," he said, "Let's go."

And they went to join the others.

A FLIGHT APART

Chapter 2

Some visitors to the Battle of Britain Memorial Flight believe they have come to see an Air Force Museum. Perhaps they came to this conclusion having seen some of the Guides! Nevertheless they are smartly disillusioned, and informed in no uncertain terms that it is a Display Flight; that all aircraft in the hangar are airworthy, and really do fly on displays in this country and abroad.

Yet the Flight has a distinctive flavour; it is not like a squadron. It has its own etiquette and customs - some might even say there is an element of the subversive about; a tradition lingering on from the days of the Second World War. One of those who might have contributed to that element was its first Adjutant, Flight Lieutenant Douglas Eke.

There was a visit in the early days - 1983 or 84 - by a very Senior Officer and various members of his staff. Afterwards the Senior Officer was invited to sign the Visitors' Book by the Flight Adjutant. Only a few pages had been used, and the Adjutant indicated the next vacant line. There was a distinct pause: then the Adjutant said, "Here, Sir, there are no special VIP's." Then turning back a page, "Oh, yes, there was one." and he pointed out the signature of the widow of Sergeant Hannah, V.C.

———————●———————

The radio call sign of the Lancaster is simply "Lancaster". There can be no confusion - there is only one. (If the Lancaster is accompanied in the air by fighter aircraft, the call sign becomes "Memorial Flight.")

On one occasion, the Lancaster was en route to St.Mawgan in Cornwall and approaching the American Air Force base at Upper Heyford. Permission is required to fly through any military air space, so the Navigator of the Lancaster - Adjutant Flt.Lt. Eke - radioed ahead, "Upper Heyford, this is Lancaster."

Upper Heyford: "Say again callsign."

Navigator: "Lancaster."

Upper Heyford: "Type of aircraft?"

Navigator: "Lancaster"

Upper Heyford: "What's a Lancaster?"

Navigator: "A four-engined, Second World War heavy bomber."

Upper Heyford: "Oh, just like our B17."

Navigator: "Yes, but a lot better."

Silence from Upper Heyford. On the Flight Deck, the conversation continued:

The Flight's Lancaster PA474 turns in for a display.

Captain to navigator: "You ought not to have said that."

Navigator to Captain: "Did I lie?"
Long pause.

Captain to navigator: "No."

—————— ◎ ——————

Flt.Lt. Eke suggests that B.B.M.F. has another claim to fame from its early days - as the only unit to have interrupted a speech by Her Majesty the Queen, and been able to prove that it was not their fault ! This dates back to the 40th anniversary of the D-day landings, 1984.

The Flight Plan called for a Flypast over the assembled eleven Heads of State at Arromanche in Normandy in the morning and a further flypast in the afternoon when they would be joined by the Navy's Historic Aircraft Flight. On the ground, Her Majesty then unveiled the D-Day Museum. The Mayor of Arromanche was to speak for two minutes: Her Majesty was to reply, and then go walkabout amongst the gathered veterans. That was the plan, and there was to be no deviation. In the air, B.B.M.F. were to continue along the coast for 10 miles before returning over Arromanche, Her Majesty and the veterans, en route for Jersey.

The French were extremely anxious about security. There was some justification with eleven Heads of State to be looked after, and to counter possible terrorist attack the whole of the Normandy coast was a mass of AAA and Surface to Air Missiles. No deviation from the agreed plan was a part of the security arrangements. All went well until the Museum.

Consider what was seen on television..

The Mayor suffered from nerves and a touch of verbosity - enough to over-run his time generously.

Her Majesty began her reply to a background accompaniment of Merlins gradually growing louder. There was to be no deviation from the plan.

People started to look up. The Duke of Edinburgh looked up. The senior RAF officer representing the Air Force Board changed colour..

Her Majesty gives up trying to speak.

The camera points vertically: there are B.B.M.F.'s aircraft exactly on time and in perfect formation overhead.

Flt.Lt. Eke points out the moral: "If you're going to have a cock-up, make sure it's a good one and you can blame someone else for it!"

The incidents related above finally lead to recognition for Flt.Lt. Eke. After his stint as the Flight Adjutant, Doug was posted to be Commanding Officer at the RAF Missile Range Unit at Aberporth on Cardigan Bay. Whilst there, he was invited as a guest to attend the Battle of Britain Open Day at RAF St Athan, where the Guest of Honour was a very senior Officer, the Air Member for Personnel. By coincidence this same very senior Officer was, and had been for some time, directly responsible for B.B.M.F. policy at the highest level and was therefore delighted to be able - during the B.B.M.F. display - to tell the rather junior Flight Lieutenant Navigator all about the Memorial Flight.

However, from the junior officer's responses it became clear that he too knew something about the Flight. "You seem to know a lot about B.B.M.F.," said the very senior officer.

"Yes, Sir, I was on the Flight and left in 1984."

"Your name?"

"Flight Lieutenant Eke, Sir"

"Oh ! You're Eke, are you!"

Fame at last!

ALL IN THE DAY'S WORK 1 - THE GUIDES

Chapter 3

It was a lovely late Spring morning in 1996. Bright, sunny with a good breeze (all airfields are windy places...); the kind of morning that lifts spirits and brings smiles to faces not always used to such muscular exercise.

The 11.00am tour party were assembled outside the Visitors' Centre. The Guide introduced himself, "My name's Nelson: I'm your Guide for the tour. Welcome to Royal Air Force Coningsby."

Nelson was not a man of Naval connection, but he was unusual for most Guides were former members of the R.A.F.; Nelson was a member of that oft-forgotten body, the Royal Observer Corps. So much has been written about the enormous advantage given to our Air Force by radar that we forget the contribution made by the members of the R. O. C. once enemy aircraft were behind the radar screen and over this country. All plots, changes of course, estimates of height had to be made by the Mark I Eyeball, and most of those belonged to Observers.

Nelson briefed his party, some dozen in number. He also asked whether anyone had connections with the Service; had flying experience, or worked in the aircraft industry. It helps to know at what level to present information, said Nelson. One man rather grudgingly admitted that he had served with the R.A.F.

"Could you tell us if you were aircrew?"

"If you wish: I flew with a Spitfire Squadron for most of the Battle of Britain....."

There was a momentary silence; then a buzz of appreciation as the rest of the party realised they had a Second World War hero in their midst.

"Marvellous," said Nelson, making a mental note that he had in that party at least one man who knew far more about Spitfires than he did! What Nelson did not know at that stage - for he had not asked - was that the two elderly gentlemen with a lady at the back of the party were from Germany.

They proceeded round the hangar, first pausing behind the Dakota - the latest acquisition - and then down past the fighter aircraft until they came to the Mark II Spitfire. This remarkable aircraft is the oldest Spitfire in flying condition, being delivered to 266 Squadron on 2 September 1940 and making her first foray into the Battle on 4 September. It is the only aircraft which actually fought in the Battle and is still flying today. Nelson invited the ex-Spitfire pilot to talk to the party. Before he could move from the extreme right of the party, a gentleman from the opposite end intervened. "I think you should be aware," he said with a strong accent, "that I am a former Luftwaffe pilot. I too fought in the Battle over England, though of course, I was flying Messerschmitt 109's..."

Nelson's intervention was immediate. "Well, then," he said, "it's time for you two to make friends," and he beckoned to both of them. "Come out here and shake hands," - an invitation both accepted. There was a little ripple of applause, and to avoid embarrassment Nelson ushered the party towards the next aircraft.

Ask Nelson what happened next and he will say he doesn't remember. "I just got on with the tour. The pair of them were somewhere in the party; they weren't listening to me, they were too busy talking to each other!"

After the tour was over, Nelson invited the two former pilots into the Crew Room where they were introduced to the other Guides, plied with coffee and questions, and supplied with paper to exchange names and addresses. Finally, they made their way over to the Car Park, the German with his arm round the Englishman's shoulders, talking and laughing. But Nelson did not see that; he was outside the Visitors' Centre, briefing the next party.

———————◉———————

Alan knew it was a Thursday afternoon; partly because his wife had reminded him that morning to put the refuse bags out (Thursday was refuse day), and partly because the Pensioners' Outing bus pulled into the Car Park.

An enterprising bus company from the Midlands was including B.B.M.F. on its Pensioners' Mystery tours, and they were always on a Thursday. Often the old folk were from an established Club and knew each other well; they had had a good lunch on the way, and after a short drive found themselves stretching their legs in the Car Park. Reaction to being shown round a collection of old aeroplanes always varied; some of the ladies preferred a nap in the coach, others wanted to sit on the grass in the sunshine and gossip, but there was always a hard core of the interested - and those who weren't sure but under no circumstances were going to be left out of whatever was going on.

'Good God' thought Alan, 'I've got the walking wounded today ! Two wheelchairs; three sticks, and a St. John's ambulance man bringing up the rear!" But they were a jolly lot and Alan soon began to enjoy the afternoon. They jostled round him, laughing, joking; feeling happily superior to those staying behind in the coach. Despite age and some infirmity they had the 'get up and go' spirit - after all this was the Battle of Britain Flight and they had all lived through that torrid summer. They were going to enjoy the afternoon.

It was customary on entering the hangar to give a short history of the Flight. He had no sooner started than he was interrupted by a tall, angular lady who demanded, "Speak up, young man! I can't hear yer.."

Alan, who would never see 65 again, beamed. He couldn't remember the last time anyone had called him, 'Young man' . He would try to respond in the same vein.

"Right," he said, raising his voice, " is this better? It's important you hear me, because when we finish I shall ask you questions and if you don't know the answers you have to stay behind and sweep the hangar floor!"

But the questioner, seventy five if she was a day, wasn't looking at Alan. She was looking over Alan's shoulder at a young RAF Corporal, six-foot, fair-haired, athletic. "Ooooh!", she said, "I could sweep the floor all night wiv him!"

Amid raucous laughter from the men, and some comments from the other ladies which no self-respecting Guide would repeat, Alan abandoned his history of the Flight and moved the party on.

But there was, he said afterwards, one golden moment. The party were grouped behind the Flight's precious Hurricane, 'Last of the Many'.

Alan was talking about its wood and canvas fuselage, when a quiet voice said, "I used to make them."

Alan wheeled round, "Who did?"

A small, insignificant figure emerged. Perhaps the last person one would notice in the group, drab, grey-haired, she repeated, "I used to make them."

"How so?"

"Well, I worked in a furniture factory in High Wycombe. We was taken over, and spent the next three years making them things." Alan encouraged her, and with gaining confidence she told how she cut the fabric, an Irish linen, into strips using things like pinking shears: how these were pasted onto the stringers - the long strips of wood that ran lengthways down the fuselage - and how the linen was then 'doped' to make the strips of linen shrink and tighten.

"Not a glamorous job," she said, "but we knew we was doing something important for the boys."

The elderly man standing next to her gave her a gentle pat on the back. She straightened and smiled as if she had waited fifty years for the recognition. He had made her afternoon.

——————⊙——————

Hurricane under construction showing (on right) the wooden stringers running lengthways down the fuselage to which the linen strips were attached.

A tour party like many others: about a dozen or more, all adult for the schools were still in session in early June. An elderly lady walked gamely but haltingly with a stick on which she leant rather heavily. A grey-haired, thick-set man hovered, his hand never far from the lady's elbow.

The party proceeded down the line of fighter aircraft with the Guide giving his customary comments. As they came to one of the Mark XIX Spitfires, the elderly man muttered, "Hmm, I didn't know they had that one here," and stooping to the lady, he asked, "Did you check that one in your Log Book?"

"Yes, dear," she replied gently, "I checked for them all."

This little exchange was overheard by the Guide, and the term 'Log Book' registered. All pilots, whether military or civil, are required to keep a Log of all flights. Details such as date; aircraft registration, time of take-off and landing, relevant airfields, all have to be recorded for every flight, and within the Service all Log Books are periodically inspected and signed by Squadron commanders. A Log Book is an important item, and in effect, a legal document.

At a suitable moment, the Guide said quietly to the couple, "I heard you mention a Log Book. Were either of you in the Royal Air Force?"

"No," replied the man, "but my wife was a qualified pilot."

"Shush now, there's no need to mention that." She tried to move on.

The Guide persisted. "I don't understand. You weren't in the Service, yet your husband asked if you'd checked a Mark XIX Spitfire in your Log."

She turned and, clearly embarrassed, told the Guide, "I was a Ferry pilot. I delivered aircraft from the factories to RAF Maintenance units - sometimes direct to squadrons. I ferried about one hundred Spitfires altogether, but I'm afraid none of these came my way."

"Well, thank you for explaining," responded the Guide, "would you like to talk to the party about flying Spits ?"

Her husband gave a short laugh. "You've done very well to get her to admit to being a Ferry pilot.

Normally she won't talk at all about it: now don't push your luck!"

Afterwards, in the Crew Room, the Guide told his colleagues about his distinguished visitor.

"Well, who was she? What was her name?" they asked.

"Good Lord, I completely forgot to ask!"

Being unaware that you have in your tour party someone who knows more about a particular aspect than you do is a not unknown hazard to Guides. It happened recently to Will.

"Whenever I take a party round, I say in my introduction - among other things, that I am an ex-Radio/radar chap. That is my expertise and I am happy to take any questions.

One day, standing in between the Hurricane and a Spitfire, someone asked why there was such a difference in the air intakes between the two types of aircraft. I really had no answer so I owned up; said I didn't know but would certainly find out at the end of the tour. Then a quiet, unassuming man at the back of the party said maybe he could help, and gave a superbly simple explanation of an obviously complex subject.   At the end of his

explanation I thanked him, and asked how he knew all that information.

'I was on the Spitfire design team,' was the reply.

I must admit to feeling about two inches high for I had talked to the party all about the Spitfire - but then......he was a very courteous fellow."

One of the more bizarre incidents to have occurred during a guided tour at the Memorial Flight involved Peter. He had just started a tour when a couple - thirties something - arrived and booked in. The normal procedure is for the tourists, having booked in at the hatch in the Crew Room, to be directed to the Visitors' Centre, from where they are collected by the Guide at the appropriate time. On this occasion, the latecomers were taken straight into the hangar where Peter had just commenced a short history of the Flight. They joined the party, having been told they could see the Visitors' Centre after the tour of the hangar was over. This was not unusual when the party was small in number and the tour only just started.

All went normally. Round the rear of the Dakota; down the side of the hangar where the fighters are lined up, and then round the corner to the tail end of the Lancaster. Peter usually made a point of talking about the rear turret and its occupant - he had a healthy regard for Rear Gunners who had perhaps the most dangerous job in a bomber crew, and were often the youngest member of that crew. It was while he was thus talking that he noticed his latecomers; they had become detached from the rest of the party (something not encouraged!), the lady sitting on the chair in the corner, her head in her hands, while her escort hovered solicitously bending over and apparently comforting her.

Now Guides are under instructions not to leave their parties unattended, so Peter completed his chat about Rear Gunners, answered a few questions and then showed the party to the Exit door with directions to the Visitors' Centre. He then went back in the hangar where the couple remained in the corner.

"Having problems? Not feeling well?" he queried. The lady remained silent, head down. Peter noticed she was shivering. Her escort mumbled something about it being very unusual; he bent over her, his words lost in the noise of the hangar.

"Look here," said Peter, "can she walk to the Visitors' Centre? We can get some water, some refreshment for her."

The lady struggled to her feet; with the man's arm around her she walked slowly, eyes averted from the aircraft, to the Exit door .

"Probably feel better now she's out in the fresh air," said the ever-helpful Guide. There was no response from either. She walked as in a dream, her arms clasped tightly round her body, her hair falling over her face. On the one occasion she looked up Peter could see that she was as white as a sheet.

Into the Visitors' Centre they went. Most of the seats at the entrance were occupied by people waiting for the next tour, and it was while casting round for somewhere for her to sit that the lady screamed. "That's him! That's him! I saw him there...." and to her companion "....don't you dare say I didn't." and she shook and sobbed inconsolably.

Now some ten paces or so inside the Visitors' Centre there is a tailor's dummy dressed in Second World War flying kit, such as was worn by bomber crews, complete in leather helmet and fur-lined boots. It was this figure that the lady had seen, and which had caused her such consternation. But, thought Peter to himself, she had not seen that figure before; they came late and were escorted straight into the hangar.

"Sorry about this," said the young man.

Bob, Guide for the next tour, came in at that moment. He had heard the commotion on his way over and misinterpreting completely said to Peter, "What the hell have you been up to?"

Then he saw the lady and exclaimed, "Good God, she looks as if she has just seen a ghost!"

"I think that's exactly what she has seen," retorted her companion. He then explained that as they were alongside the Lancaster, Peter had made the point that while it appears a large aircraft from the outside, it is in fact very cramped inside. Normal entry is up the short ladder to the hatch just ahead of the tail unit........... Following what he was saying the lady had looked at the hatch and apparently seen a figure dressed in full Second World War flying kit, standing stooped in the hatchway. At that time she did not know what that kit meant; she had never seen it. Only when she saw the tailor's dummy did she fully comprehend what she had seen. Her companion had tried to talk her out of it, but that only made things worse; she had seen him - he was really there - and she knew, she just knew, he was a figure from the past.

There was no explanation. Apparently, she had never 'seen' any figure before, not had any kind of similar experience, said her companion. "Perfectly normal person," he declared. In time, she became more composed and together they left. As they passed the Guides' Crew Room, the young man waved cheerily enough.

"Well," said Bob later," there can't be a ghost for that aircraft - didn't see war service. And if it's the Station ghost, what's it doing in the doorway of the Lanc?"

Oh, yes, Coningsby has its ghost...........but that's another story altogether.

OPERATION
MANNA

Chapter 4

In 1995, Mick, short, dapper, bespectacled, was a Guide at the Battle of Britain Memorial Flight at Coningsby. On a May morning, a party of some half dozen Dutch businessmen was booked in. Mick had been asked to take them round the Lancaster and was introduced as a man who had flown on Operation Manna - the 50th anniversary of which had recently been marked both here and in the Netherlands. During his talk about Lancaster PA474 which towered above the little group, Mick mentioned that besides bringing devastation to the German heartlands Lancaster squadrons had turned their skills to humanitarian tasks such as dropping food supplies and bringing home released prisoners of war.

One of the Dutchmen pressed forward. "Did you drop food on the racecourse outside the Hague?"

Mick said that he had.

"And were you there on the first day?"

Again Mick nodded.

"Then I saw you! I was there too.......I was ten........My mother and I had heard you were coming and we had waited since dawn. We were cold and wet and unbelievably hungry..........we heard you first........we were looking too high. Then you came and people around me were shouting and sobbing, knowing then that we were

(Photograph courtesy of Mick Bridger)

The crew of Lancaster A-Able, No 153 Squadron, R.A.F. Scampton, April 1945. Mick just manages to get into the photograph, kneeling, left.

going to stay alive. I have waited fifty years to meet one of the men who saved us."

And he walked out and shook Mick by the hand warmly.

"Tell me......how did it feel to you..... to be dropping food instead of bombs? Did it not make you feel good?"

Mick, embarrassed, scratched his ear and fifty-year old memory. "No, not really. We were too shit-scared to feel anything on that first drop.........."

———————⊙———————

In April 1945, Mick, five feet nothing, from the east end of London, was Bomb Aimer in the crew of Lancaster A-Able of No 153 Squadron based at Scampton, a few miles north of Lincoln. For years, aircraft of Bomber Command had pounded away at Nazi Germany, destroying industrial plant, disrupting communications, weakening morale. Now a different task was about to present itself; difficult to execute and daunting for the crews for whom there was no respite.

By April 1945, a desperate situation had developed in the Netherlands. Dutch Resistance had shown unrelenting hostility throughout to the occupying German forces; in September 1944 Dutch transport workers had gone on strike in order to assist Allied forces during the Battle of Arnhem. In retaliation the Germans placed an embargo on the movement of food in the densely populated urban areas, and in the bitter winter of 44/45 fuel supplies had virtually run out. Yet the Germans had clung desperately to this territory if for no other reason than that the V2 Rocket attacks against London could be launched only from their Dutch sites. As the Allied armies drove into the heart of Germany in March and April, Holland was cut off and the majority of the Dutch people faced starvation.

Back in London, there had been attempts - not least by Queen Wilhelmina - to persuade Bomber Command to drop food supplies, but this was not as easy as it might sound. Only by flying at very low level and slow speed could food be dropped successfully, and under those conditions the bombers would be sitting-duck targets for the German anti-aircraft gunners. Only if the Germans agreed not to open fire could the operation be mounted and there were many valid objections to any sort of deal with the enemy. However, by mid-April the situation in Holland was judged critical and General Eisenhower, the Supreme Allied Commander, forced the issue by contacting the German Commander and on 24 April announced his intention to bring relief to the Dutch people. There followed an interchange of messages; the details of the flights - dates, times, courses, speeds, heights, were all given to the German Command but when the Delegations from both sides met formally on the 28th none of the necessary guarantees was forthcoming.

From the latest reports it was agreed that there could be no further delays. Dire warnings were issued to the Germans of the consequences should they interfere in the air or on the ground..........and so began Operation Manna.

On the morning of 29 April, 153 Squadron was called to Briefing. They were to drop food on Duindigt Racecourse just north of The Hague; the Dropping Zone would be marked on the ground with a white cross and red smoke markers would be dropped by Mosquito aircraft prior to the arrival of the Lancasters. Take-off for the first of 153's aircraft was to be at 11.25 hours.

"They're mad!" thought Mick and the rest of A-Able's crew...........several crews are pretty new ....too many youngsters for this job. The weather's awful.........can't see the end of the runway........Met. man says it's clear over the D.Z. and you know how often he's right!

"They're all bloody mad," muttered Mick as, encumbered by his kit, he clambered up the ladder into the belly of A-Able.

What none of the crews knew was that no signed agreement had been received from the Germans. If they chose to fire, no Lancaster had the remotest chance of survival.

As well as making the actual drop, Mick - on low level - assisted the navigator by map-reading from the glazed nose of the Lancaster, relaying sitings via the internal radio.

"Can't see a damn thing!" said Mick helpfully as they crossed the English coast at Southwold; then out over the North Sea and made landfall near Rotterdam dead on track. This part of the sortie had been flown at 1,000 feet; coming in over the Dutch coast the weather lifted, indeed just as the Met. man had forecast, and Mick could see the German A.A. batteries waiting for them. The hairs on his back rose as the guns swung and followed the Lancaster round.............but they did not fire.

A Bomb Aimer was a man of many parts: he was also a gunner responsible for the operation of the front turret and Mick made sure his ammunition was live and the guns cocked. As if reading his thoughts, the pilot barked over the R.T., "Don't let fly - that's just what they want!" Mick could see the German troops quite clearly and he was convinced they were looking straight at him.

By now they had tracked north up the designated corridor towards The Hague and the Dropping Zone. Mick found it difficult to map-read; so many features which would have been visible under normal conditions were just not there - everything was covered by water. He had never seen flooding like it; the land was devastated. The Germans had used the sluice gates as a form of defence to hamper Allied movements; Mick saw people clinging to rooftops and thought to himself, "I'll bet the D.Z.'s a bit soggy - wonder if the recipe says, 'Mix with water'."

The Lancaster had about a ton of food on board, carried in sacks made of jute or hessian - about the size of cement or sandbags. They were strung on cords down the length of the bomb bay so that they would drop rapidly in sequence...

Then they saw the D.Z.; not clearly because the smoke from the Mosquito flares had not yet dispersed. They were already down to low level; down even further ("Christ!" thought Mick, "we're below 100 feet - thank God Holland's flat!") He had already heard the pilot order 25 deg. flap and haul the speed back to 120 knots.

"Bomb doors open."

He could see vividly people waving; some had brought out previously hidden flags, some had tablecloths - anything they could find. The crews had been told at Briefing that the Dutch had been warned to stay clear of the D.Z., but Mick could see they were running all over it, rushing for sacks that had already been dropped. Some had burst on impact and the contents were being scooped up into the mouths of the starving men, women and children.

For this Operation, 153 had been issued with specially constructed, hand-held 'bomb' sights: Mick lined up and as the pilot held the Lancaster low, straight and level the sacks of food slid from the bomb bay.

Thus far there had been no interference from German troops but A-Able's crew were taking no chances. Up came the flaps; up went the speed, but A-Able stayed down. On their way out, Mick found himself looking up at a windmill! It was just before 3.00pm when Mick's Lancaster touched down on the runway at Scampton from which she had taken off some three and a half hours before. Mick and his crew were to make another three sorties on Operation Manna, the last on 4 May - just four days before the final wartime operation of Bomber Command.

The second drop was at Rotterdam and on the way out Mick's Lancaster sought admirable cover from possible belligerent German gunners by flying down one of the main wide streets of that city. Like a photograph printed on his memory were the balustrades he could see on top of matching buildings that framed the entrance to the street. There were people rushing out of the buildings waving and cheering, and then ducking down as the Lancaster roared only feet above their heads. The crew slipped sweets and bars of chocolate from their rations out of the side windows.

But there was one important difference about these subsequent sorties: assurance (for what it was worth) had been received from the German Command that there would be no interference with these mercy flights. On that first sortie, there was

Mick looking up at the Bomb-Aimer's position in Lancaster PA474, July 1997.

no such assurance: crews flew without any such safeguard and with only the certainty that if the German gunners chose to fire then they would not return home. It needed a special kind of courage to fly to save life, rather than destroy it.

———————— ⊙ ————————

Sometime in the late Sixties, Mick was on business in Rotterdam on behalf of his firm. At one point he was in a taxi with several others en route between meetings. Leaning forward he spoke through the partition and asked the driver to change the route.

"Diversion," explained Mick to the others. "There's a big, wide street and at the end several buildings - sort of matching - on either side of the road. Tall they are, with a stone balustrade running round the tops."

Sure enough, after a few minutes, there were the buildings; tall, imposing, very Dutch. Mick stopped the taxi and got out. Slowly he craned his head, this way and that. Finally, stock still, he gazed down that wide thoroughfare. Then he got back into the taxi.

"Thought you said you'd never been here before?" queried one of his companions.

"No more I have," responded Mick, and then added enigmatically, "and the last time I saw them I was looking up at them."

And he would say no more.

JOINING
UP

Chapter 5
In the beginning - Norman

The talk had turned to the early days: of Reception Centres; Initial Training Wings, Mustering and Trade Training.

"I think I hold an Air Force record," said Norman, "at least I've never met anyone else who didn't do square-bashing."

"How d'you get away with that, then?"

Norman was a Lincolnshire lad, born at Thorpe St. Peter out near the coast. He joined up in April 1940 at the Reception Centre at Cardington, the old airship station in Bedfordshire. There he had his jabs and was kitted out. When the question of his trade came up, there were no options.

"You are going to be sent for training as an armourer."

"Why an armourer, Sir?"

"Because we're desperately short of armourers, that's why."

If Norman thought he might re-muster to another trade while doing his square-bashing, again he was given no option. Next day he was posted to Manby.

"Join the Air Force and see the world! And they post me back to Lincolnshire! " When he reached Manby he discovered that was where all armourers were trained, or were supposed to be for on the second night he was put on Guard Duty and issued with a rifle. "I'd never held a rifle in my life, let alone know how to fire it." When he asked what he had to do on Guard Duty he was told, "You patrol the perimeter of the airfield, Airman." and he thought it prudent not to ask what he should do with the rifle. So Norman, an airman with some five days' service, walked round the perimeter of R.A.F. Station, Manby, all night and kept his head down.

The armourer's course lasted six weeks, after which Norman was posted to Church Fenton to join a Squadron which was in the process of being formed from American nationals who had come over to this country and joined our Air Force. They became known as 71 - the first Eagle Squadron. Almost immediately, the Squadron was posted en bloc to Kirton Lindsey - back to Lincolnshire again, thought Norman. And perhaps he regretted not doing square-bashing when he was detailed as one of the Bearer Party for the coffin of the first American casualty of Second World War, a pilot killed accidentally on a training flight. He hoped he was smart enough to do justice to the solemnity of the occasion.

Then Norman left Lincolnshire. In April 1941, he was posted to the Middle East, arriving at Ismailia in June. There he looked after the armament of the Hurricanes of an Operational Training Unit. For safety, the unit moved quickly to Khartoum, and there the unit - and Norman - remained for three long years.

In the Spring of 44, Norman moved to Naples en route for England and home. He was actually on the boat when his name was called and he found himself in a shore Adjutant's Office.

"You're going out to the Far East," he was told.

"Why is that , Sir?"

"Because we're desperately short of armourers in the Far East, that's why".

What Norman actually said at that point is not known, but eventually there was a concession.

"Look here, tell you what, 6 Squadron's just down the road. They're a Hurricane lot. I'll attach you to them until there's a space on the next boat. O.K.?"

"Fine," said Norman, but it took another year for that space to become available.

The boat docked in Liverpool, and all Air Force personnel were taken immediately to the Holding Unit at Blackpool. Norman's first action was to rush into the nearest phone box and telephone home. Well, he tried but no one answered, nor did the Operator; the phone just wasn't working. He complained to the first person who would listen: "Well, of course it ain't working - nobody is - it's VE day ! Come and have a beer!"

It was then Norman discovered he had only Lire in his pocket!

Towards the End - John

It was a golden Spring, April and May on the English Riviera. Cambridge University Air Squadron of 1944/45 was now fully mustered and stationed at Air Crew Reception Centre, Torquay. Bliss it was in that time to be alive. Quarters were in requisitioned hotels. Food (double civilian rations) was superb. The daily duties comprised Drill, P.T., exercise and perchance one Lecture during which most dozed gently. Interspersed with this intensely physical routine undertaken in Flights of approximately thirty men were individual details for testing - medical, dental, aptitude, interview and so on.

There were a handful of officers; they presented as remote, cardboard figures. Our daily life, and indeed the whole tradition of the Service lay in the palm of Flight Sergeant Jones. Tall and well-proportioned, carrying no surplus weight; a fine figure of a man, possessed of a rich deep voice with just a hint of artificial gentility: a "Keep quiet down there", enunciated in Raymond Massey tones could still a whole Flight.

It was on a fine afternoon that John was returning to base following a visit to the dentist as part of the individual duties. The Flight was at that hour doing P.T. on the grass in front of the hotel, entrance to which from the road was always made from the rear. Would it then be possible to hide until the hour of P.T. was over? This ignoble thought had no sooner entered John's head than the figure of Flight Sergeant Jones suddenly appeared from the rear of the hotel.

"Cadet. What are you doing?"

"I've been to the dentist, Flight Sergeant."

"Oh. Do you feel alright, lad? Would you like to come into the Guardroom for a cup of tea?"

"Thank you very much, Flight Sergeant."

How many did you have out, lad?"

"I didn't have any out, Flight Sergeant. I had two fillings."

"Fillings ! Fillings ! Fillings are f*** all . Go and do some P.T.!"

Ten or more years on, and John was attending a course in London with the RAFVR. In charge of discipline was Warrant Officer Jones.

"Excuse me, Mr Jones. You were my Flight Sergeant at Torquay in '45"

"Ah, yes, indeed. You must have come from Cambridge, Sir."

ALL IN THE
DAY'S WORK 2 -
THE GUIDES

Chapter 6

It was Abraham Lincoln, in a speech back in 1860, who asked, "What is conservatism? Is it not adherence to the old and tried, against the new and untried?" One visitor to the Battle of Britain Memorial Flight would have given positive applause to the question.

He was in a party in the summer of 1996, on a day when the Lancaster PA474 was to take part in a mid-week display. Normally, displays and fly-pasts take place at weekends, but occasionally a mid-week event is considered sufficiently significant for MoD to authorise a flight. On this particular occasion, start-up was timed for late morning, and Bill had collected his party from the Visitors' Centre with the Lancaster outside the hangar and the ground crew standing-by. "Right," said Bill, "we'll go straight down to the hard-standing and watch the Lancaster depart." In the sunshine, the party trooped down to the viewing area adjacent to where the Lancaster stood. On the way, Bill chatted with members of his party and learnt that one elderly fellow was an ex-Second World War Halifax pilot. Bill chatted about the Lancaster, tactfully omitting any comparison between that and the Halifax, when out came the crew for the day.

Smartly dressed in their black aircrew suits, carrying kit and the heavy helmets, they climbed the short ladder just in front of the tail unit and disappeared into the fuselage. There was something unusual about one crew member

though; she was clearly female. As the short blond -haired figure turned in the doorway, the former heavy bomber pilot gasped, "Good God, a woman in the crew!"

In fact, she was not; she was a W.R.A.F. engine fitter with the rank of Corporal, and it was she who had done the Daily Inspection on the Lancaster's Merlin engines that morning. Often, however, members of the ground crew fly with the aircraft; an overnight away-stay means an inspection next morning and that has to be done by the ground crew. It is also a way of rewarding them for their hard work and long hours during the display season. Ask from what position you have the best view and you will be told - the mid-upper turret. So, a few moments later and the W.R.A.F. Corporal's head appeared in the glazing of the turret as the first of the Merlins crackled into life.

There was a howl from the former wartime pilot, "Oh, no! I don't believe it! Not a bloody gunner!"

By the time all four engines were running, checks made, chocks pulled from the massive tyres, and the Lancaster had trundled round the perimeter track and disappeared from view, most of Bill's party were under no illusions about one member's views on women in Service aircraft; what he would have done had he been asked to have a woman in his crew; what trades he thought women were fit for, and what indeed was the Service coming to..........

Bill was thankful to be able to lead his party into the hangar and show them some fighter aircraft, powered by Rolls-Royce's beloved Merlin. At least that was a piece of engineering old and tried and not in the least controversial. It was also a piece of kit which Bill knew inside and out ....for Bill had been a Halton 'Brat'.

———————⊙———————

It is generally accepted that Lord Trenchard was the architect, and indeed, father of the Royal Air Force. He knew that an efficient Air Force needed not only fine aircraft and well-trained crews to fly them but equally vital were first-rate ground crews to maintain the machines. So he devised and inaugurated the Apprentices Training School based at Halton in Buckinghamshire.

The School took lads of 16 years of age and gave them not just an education but one of the best technical training courses available anywhere. From the School , in time, came a stream of engine fitters, airframe riggers, electricians, instrument fitters - all the trades which the modern aircraft needed to be kept in sound flying condition anywhere where the Air Force was called upon to serve. Trenchard once referred to the youngsters at Halton as his 'Brats' and the name stuck.

Bill entered Halton in 1936 ; by 1941 he had been commissioned as an Engineering Officer, and served for the rest of the war with Spitfire Squadrons. What he did not know about the Merlin was not really worth knowing.

———————⊙———————

It was knowledge which stood him in good stead when tricky questions arose. During 1996, there was an official visit to Coningsby by a party of Czechoslovak Air Force personnel, and Bill was asked to take them round B.B.M.F. There was a Wing Commander in charge; an Engineer, and three or four pilots. They showed much interest in the Spitfires as they were all part of a Czech. fighter Squadron; there were many questions and one which made Bill think was asked by the Wing Commander, "How much fuel did a Spitfire have?"

Bill did not have to think about 90 gallons - that was automatic, but he realised that his answer would have to be in litres. A quick mental calculation, and he replied, "About 450 litres."

The Wing Commander raised his eyebrows : "I use more than that just starting up! ....but of course, we are flying MiG 29's."

———————⊙———————

Another Continental visitor revealed himself as an ex - Luftwaffe pilot. Bill was impressed: "You speak very good English!"

"So I bloody-well should do," he replied, "I spent five years in a Prisoner of War camp in England!"

The visitor explained that he had been on a Messerschmitt 109 Squadron and on one occasion in what later became known as the Battle of

Messerschmitt Bf 109. A captured example, restored and re-painted in Royal Air Force colours, flown for evaluation purposes.

Britain, he had been caught up in a massive dog-fight over Ramsgate. With a Spitfire on his tail he made the mistake of crossing in front of his No 2 just as the latter opened fire, and was thus shot down by a member of his own Luftwaffe Squadron.

He baled out, and spent 36 hours in a dinghy in the inhospitable English Channel - hoping all the time that he would be picked up by a German rescue launch. Finally he was fished out, but by a British vessel.

"No hard feelings?" asked Bill.

"None whatever...." responded the former prisoner.

———————— ⊙ ————————

"Talking about Me 109's...." Bill was in reverie mode.

"I was on 72 Squadron.....about August '43 this would be. We had just gone into Sicily and taken over an abandoned German airfield. Well, it was really a landing strip - no more - but abandoned at one end of the strip we found two unserviceable 109's. I'd often wanted to have a good look at one, and we thought that if we could get them back in flying condition it would be a useful exercise for our lads to see what they could do. Assess their strengths and weaknesses for ourselves.

Well, in time we managed, and two of our intrepid chaps took them off. No 1 got into all sorts of trouble, and with the coolant temperature off the top of the clock, he decided to bale out - came down in the sea and was picked up by Air Sea Rescue. Now this chap had already had to bale out of a Spitfire, and he may be the only R.A.F. pilot who achieved the double - baling out of both a Spit and a 109!

No 2 had a more successful flight - that is until he came into land. All hell was let loose - tracer cracking over the airstrip at 50'. You see, we'd forgotten to tell our American friends down the road what we were up to; they saw this aircraft with

Black crosses on final approach - couldn't believe their eyes - threw everything at it. Didn't hit it though, and the pilot landed safely."

A pause.

"You know, there'd have been uproar if the Powers That Be got to know half what we got up to."

Another pause.

"Well, occasionally, they did."

Still in reverie mode; still with 72 Squadron; now in Italy. "If you fly to Naples today," Bill continues, "you'll land at Capodachino. When we got there in October '43, it was a small grass airfield littered with Junkers 52's in various stages of disrepair and damage. It had one battered hangar, and.......oh, yes, there was Vesuvius on the final approach to land. It's still there; good thing - keeps the pilots awake.

You know, in those days we used to liberate things.......things such as motor cars. At Capodachino we found a magnificent Lancia: the Germans thought they had immobilised their abandoned vehicles by taking all the wheels off, heaping them into a large pile and then blowing the lot up. But they had not bargained for the versatility of the Royal Air Force Trolley-acc.

Remember them? They littered war-time airfields: a simple trolley full of accumulators with a lead, mounted on two, tyred ,19 inch wheels. Trundle it alongside your aircraft; plug in to the electrical system and use the power of the accumulators for your cold start. Just like modern jump-leads. Wonderful idea. Anyway, four wheels from trolley-accs somehow found their way to a neighbouring R.E.M.E. unit who kindly modified them to fit the Lancia, which subsequently became the Squadron runabout. Unfortunately, we didn't enjoy it for long. We had a passing visit from A.V.M. Sir Harry Broadhurst, who said we were doing jolly well; saw the Lancia and promptly commandeered it for his own use!"

After coffee, and Bill had reached Klagenfelt in southern Austria. "Of course, by this time it was after VE day and the pressure was off. We could relax a bit - the pace was slower. Klagenfelt was one of the Luftwaffe's training stations. They used to start flying training on gliders, you know; different from us. There the place was stocked with Messerschmitt 108's - lovely little aeroplane -, and Storches, and hundreds of gliders. We had this ambition to get everybody up in gliders, and by the time we left 90% of the Squadron - the clerks and the cooks and the orderlies - had managed to go solo. Great stuff - that was real liberation."

THE NIGHT OF
3/4 MARCH

Chapter 7

In 1992, Bob, tall, smart, angular, was a Guide at the Battle of Britain Memorial Flight - as he had been since it opened its doors to the public in 1986. One of the more senior members, Bob gave his time to organising the Guides' social activities (often at the Packet Inn) and occasional expeditions to other centres of aviation interest, as well as taking a full share of parties round the hangar.

On this particular day, Bob's party was nothing out of the ordinary. He proceeded at a steady pace down the side of the hangar and it was only at the far end where Lancaster PA474 reposed in majesty that Bob noticed a heightening of interest on the part of two elderly couples in the party. After the tour, Bob lead his party to the Visitors' Centre where there were static exhibits and one could purchase a variety of souvenirs, from large framed prints for those with memories to pencils and rubbers for smaller enthusiasts.

Bob soon got into conversation with the two elderly couples. The ladies were sisters whose brother had been killed in a Lancaster. They knew it had crashed somewhere near Alford, and they knew the date - the night of 3/4 March 1945. Then early in 1992 they happened to read Simon Parry's book, "Intruders over Britain" in which he identifies their brother's aircraft and states that it crashed at

In the early hours
of March 4th, 1945,
Lancaster PB476 (PH - "Y")
of No. 12 Squadron,
R.A.F. Wickenby,
crashed near this spot,
the victim of
a Luftwaffe intruder.

This memorial is placed here, on
the 50th anniversary of the crash,
to commemorate the crew members
who died.

Flying Officer	N.A. Ansdell	Pilot
Flying Officer	A. Hunter	Navigator
Flying Officer	A.G. Heath	Bomb Aimer
Sergeant	R.F.D. Schafer	Flight Engineer
Sergeant	R.O. Parry	Wireless Operator
Sergeant	A.R. Walker	Mid Upper Gunner
Sergeant	W. Mellor	Rear Gunner

IN GRATEFUL REMEMBRANCE

(Photograph Courtesy of Mrs M. Astbury)

Memorial Stone to the crew of Lancaster PB476 at Ulceby Cross Hill.

Weekly Cross. It was this more precise location which had lead them to Lincolnshire to seek out the places associated with their brother.

Bob stopped and thought, for the date stirred something in his memory........

He suggested Ulceby Cross (Weekly does not exist) giving the sisters and their husbands appropriate directions.........a couple of names and addresses.........

Guide Bob with Mrs Astbury, her sister and husband, in the Visitors' Centre.

At home Bob consulted diaries and notebooks - just to make sure.

Later he told his fellow Guides :

"It all came back - that night of 3rd and 4th March '45. By midnight I was safely tucked up in a warm bed where we lived then near Alford; of course I was still a schoolboy at that time. Shortly afterwards the peace of the night was shattered by the roar of aircraft engines and the sound of gunfire. Mind you, that sort of noise was not uncommon hereabouts during the war, but on that night it was so loud it woke many people.

The following morning my father, who had been out and about very early, told me about an aircraft which had crashed at Ulceby Cross hill. Like a shot I was off; collected a friend and off on our bikes we went to see what we could find. Going up the hill towards Ulceby, we saw and picked up several spent 20mm cannon shell cases; this we thought was no ordinary crash. At the crossroads where the road divides for Spilsby and Harrington, our way was barred by both civil and RAF police. 'No,' they said. 'not even two lads on their bikes could go any further.'

We dutifully turned around and when out of sight ditched our bikes and took to the hedgerows on foot. We weren't going to let a minor detail like that deter us from reaching our objective. We managed to get within a couple of hundred yards of the main crash site - rather damp as we were standing in a dyke peering through a hedge. There was wreckage strewn over a very large field - hardly any bits looked like recognisable aircraft parts, at least from where we were standing. We learnt later that the bits were all that remained of a Lancaster and that all the crew had been killed.

Later still, we were told that the aircraft was another victim of Operation Gisela. This was when German long-range night fighters infiltrated the returning Allied bomber stream, taking no action until one of the bombers descended and prepared to land. In the circuit and on finals, the bomber crew were almost home, relaxed and unwary. Then the night fighter struck: the target was easy and too low for the crew to bale out successfully. Of course, our lads were warned of this ploy, but it was not always possible to distinguish between another bomber about to land and an enemy aircraft, especially after perhaps nine hours in the air under hazardous conditions. Apparently twenty of our aircraft were lost that night, of which the Ulceby Cross wreckage was one.

Relatives of the crew of PB476 at the dedication of the Memorial.

D'you know, I'd forgotten all about that until she mentioned the 3rd and 4th of March......"

———⊙———

About a week later, Bob received the following letter :

30.9.92   Stafford

Dear Bob,

It was most fortuitous for us to have you as our Guide at Battle of Britain Memorial Flight last week and to talk to you in the museum shop afterwards where we told you that we lost our brother in a Lancaster on the night of 3/4 March 1945. You were able to tell us that you thought it was at Ulceby Cross and that you yourself as a boy went to the crash site.

After leaving you we went over there and then to visit Alford. Thanks to you we now have a clear picture of the area, we assumed hopefully that no member of the local population would have been injured. We discovered much, and our next visit was to Wickenby. It was very moving for Jean and myself to see where they flew from on that awful night. Bill had been at Wickenby only since the 27th of February. Then we went to Lincoln Cathedral to see the Services' Chapel, and our final visit was to East Kirkby which we thought was a superb tribute to all members of the Royal Air Force.

Our stay in Lincolnshire was all too brief. We hope to come again.

On behalf of us all, thank you.

Yours sincerely,

Madeleine Astbury

———⊙———

They did come again.

In March 1995, fifty years on, Bob and the two sisters, together with their husbands, the Station Commander of RAF Coningsby and the Officer Commanding Battle of Britain Memorial Flight., stood beside each other at Ulceby Cross at a Service to remember the seven airmen who died in Lancaster PB476, and to unveil a Memorial Stone at the site of the crash.

Notes.

Sergeant William Mellor, Rear Gunner of PB476, is buried in the village churchyard at Hatherton, close by the church in which he sang as a choirboy.

Simon Parry's book, "Intruders over Britain" includes a chapter on the events of the night of 3/4 March 1945.

Rev. I.Haythorne has written the story of the crash of PB476 in his book, "The Gisela Tragedy" pub. New Covenant Books, 1995.

FOLLOWING FATHER'S FOOTSTEPS

Chapter 8

It was rehearsal day.

Fifty years ago, the Battle had been fought out in the skies over southern England during those glorious summer and autumn days; a battle which we could not afford to lose. As one Guide put it to his party, "If we had lost, this country would have been invaded and the history of western Europe would have been very different."

Now there was to be a celebratory Fly-past over London in which the Flight was to take a major part, joined by squadrons flying such diverse aircraft as Hercules and Jaguar, Nimrod and Hawk, Canberra and Phantom. To co-ordinate this procession was a headache, and a rehearsal was felt necessary to achieve the required standards of precision. But not over London.

The 'honour' of acting as Buckingham Palace was given to the Simulator Unit at RAF Station, Wittering, and everything - route, timings, heights - followed from that. At Coningsby, aircraft of the Flight had been checked and stood ready for Start-up. The Flight's C.O., Squadron Leader Colin Paterson, lead his crew out to the Lancaster, and a careful observer would have noticed something unusual - an extra member. A large man with the bulk of middle-age about him, John Chatterton climbed the short ladder and began to make his way forward to the flight deck. To younger men this is something of an obstacle course; to John it was

more, and to negotiate the main spar was formidable. While the crew strapped in and began their checks, John stood behind the pilots: comparisons were inevitable - for John had flown Lancasters before; in fact he had completed 30 wartime operations with 44 Squadron from Dunholme Lodge.

Pilot's cockpit of Lancaster PA474.

Now he stood in Lancaster PA474, and one or two things didn't seem quite right; it didn't smell right for a start. He remembered the smell of wartime Lancasters; a heady mixture of 100 octane petrol, human sweat, and Elsanol. This Lancaster was clean; sterile even; and the crew now - more professional than wartime men. John heard the checklist being read out and acknowledged. He noted with approval that the starboard inner engine was still started first - that gets the generators going, and even more important - the compressor for the brakes. As they taxied out, the hiss of the air brakes brought back so many memories.......But no; he was not allowed to stay there for the take-off. He was politely escorted back to the Wireless Operator's position and strapped in. 'Quite right!' he admitted ruefully; but he also admitted that, given half a chance, he would have stayed - for the co-pilot was his son.

John was a Lincolnshire lad born and bred. He joined the Royal Air Force in January 1941 and despite volunteering for aircrew was rejected (due to tone-deafness) and trained as an armourer. Repeated requests to transfer to flying training eventually succeeded at the hands of a sympathetic Medical Officer, and John arrived in Arizona to be trained under a scheme whereby American civilians used military aircraft to turn British rookies into competent pilots after 200 hours flying.

John's first 'instructor' on Primary training was a round, tubby 'old' man of about 50, who soon made it clear to his four students he had definite views about flying. "I don't believe in any instruments except the oil temperature gauge," he told John firmly. To explain this unorthodox approach, the instructor said that he had been a bush pilot flying in and out of the gold mines in the Yukon River area. The first thing after landing was to drain the entire engine oil; the following morning the last thing was to replace the oil which had been heated in a pan over an open fire and start the engine before the oil froze solid. Despite this peculiarity, the 'old' man gave his pupils a sound start by teaching them to fly their Stearmans by the seat of their pants.

Then they moved on to the Basic course flying Vultee Valiants. Their 'instructor' for this part was also unorthodox in that he didn't like flying above 100 feet. Whilst low flying can be enormous fun, it can be dangerous - especially for a half-trained pilot. But this instructor was good; he made his living as a crop duster!

Then on to the final, Advanced Course on Harvards, where John's instructor was aged 18. His unlikely background was that his mother was a minor Hollywood starlet who had bought her son an aeroplane when a raw teenager and he had proved himself an absolute natural. The same analogy can be made for some people in water - they swim like fishes; any pilot knows that some find the air their natural element. He was the icing on John's flying training cake.

Back to the UK, and John found himself destined

for heavy aircraft. Via Oxfords and Whitleys, he completed the Heavy Conversion course at Swinderby and arrived with his crew at Dunholme Lodge in October 1943. His real war was about to begin.

————————⊙————————

Did John think as he sat in the Wireless Operator's seat in PA474 as it trundled down the Coningsby runway of his own crew of nearly fifty years ago? Much has been made of the cosmopolitan nature of wartime Bomber Command crews; John's crew was no exception, though in one respect they had a similarity problem - there were four Johns! Pilot John had become used in Arizona to being 'Johnny'; Navigator John became 'Jack'; Wireless Operator John - being a Scot - naturally became 'Jock'; but then the Rear Gunner was also a Scot. However, as he was smaller in stature than the Wireless Op., there was no difficulty in his name; he just became 'Wee Jock'. Otherwise they conformed: the Flight Engineer was a Londoner; the Navigator a Welshman; the Bomb Aimer was a Geordie, while the Mid-Upper gunner was an 18 year-old Canadian, who soon gained a reputation for having a girl in every village round about Dunholme Lodge.

————————⊙————————

They completed their tour of 30 operations. They flew on the notorious Nuremburg* raid, but saw little of the death and destruction that wiped out one in eight of the bombers in the main stream. John's was a 'wind-finder' crew who flew at the front of the stream supporting the pathfinders.

They did eight Berlin trips: long, cold, dull, with moments of intense excitement. John admits that most of his operations have now merged into single memories ; it has become difficult to recall all but one, and that particular trip will remain very clear in his memory.

They went out over Selsey Bill. Were the Navy particularly touchy that night? He will never know, but suddenly there was a tremendous 'Crump' above the aircraft, and he felt a blow on the top of his head. The perspex cover had gone, and he was left with the prospect of a very cold and draughty flight - and one hell of a headache.

Over the target, their Lancaster was nearly rammed head-on by a German night-fighter, a Focke Wulf 190. Neither saw the other until the very last minute, but it was close: John felt the air impact rock the Lancaster as the 190 came and went just over their heads.

On the way home, John and his crew managed to find the only thunderstorm over Germany. St. Elmo's fire was interesting; then came the icing and almost immediately the controls froze solid.

Then the lightning strike. John is not sure to this day whether the Lancaster turned right over, but in cloud a pilot needs his instruments and all except the "Turn and Bank" were useless as a result of the violent manoeuvre. With this one instrument John regained some measure of control, but it was not until the airspeed indicator unfroze that he realised they were diving at some 330 mph! With the help of the engineer the Lancaster was finally brought level; but they were still in cloud and had no idea of their direction - the compass was useless.

When they finally broke out of cloud, the Navigator climbed into the astrodome and found Polaris: they were heading south! John is fond of saying that the stars saved his life that night: the navigator was able to take star-shots and give him a course to steer for England and safety. However, there were still problems: the lightning had put the radio out of action and with no perspex cover all the 'flimsies' (details of emergency airfields, codesigns, etc) had been sucked out of the cockpit. So they used Sandra.

Sandra was the use of searchlights on the coast to give direction, by swinging over and down, pointing on the line of a serviceable airfield. Coming in low over the sea, John and his crew were 'directed' by Sandra to Little Snoring in Norfolk. Once able to identify the airfield, and assured by the Engineer that sufficient fuel remained, they set course over the waters of the Wash for home at Dunholme Lodge. Once the Bomb-Aimer had identified the Wainfleet range, John called Dunholme on the R T, and at the third attempt heard faintly "Hello Y - Yorker; base is closed, land at Spilsby." John turned to starboard.

Into the circuit for landing; downwind; turning finals, and the Engineer quietly over the inter-comm, "Are you going to put the wheels down, Skipper?" 'Must have been that bang on the head', thought John as he operated the undercarriage control. Then two red lights. Round again. The emergency compressed air system had to be used to change the red lights to green. But only one changed colour. What John and the crew did not know was that there was a microswitch fault and that both wheels were firmly locked down; instead John held his breath as they turned Finals for the landing.

Then Spilsby on the radio: "We've an aircraft pranged on landing; it's blocking the runway. Divert to Coningsby......divert to Coningsby."

John didn't bother to raise the wheels - just flew with them down. Into the circuit; flaps down with compressed air.   On Finals, and even his crew thought it was one of his better landings!

"Yes,' thought John as Lancaster PA474 turned on

Lancaster PA474 outside B.B.M.F.'s hangar.

Finals after the rehearsal, 'I've landed at Coningsby before."

In the fullness of time, back in civilian life, John married and he and his wife raised three children. John says he has had three careers: as an RAF pilot; as a Lecturer in Agricultural Engineering, and as a farmer. His children have followed him; Jennifer is farming; Marion into teaching, and Mike into the RAF. As a former Shackleton man, Mike is especially suited to the Lancaster and it was no secret that he wished to follow father's footsteps.

And has John flown in B.B.M.F.'s Lancaster since rehearsal day?
"Yes," he says, "I had three of my old crew with me, and my son as Skipper this time!"
This was 1992, and John had been able to contact his Bomb-Aimer, the Flight Engineer, and the Rear Gunner, Wee Jock. "And you know, it was the day after his 83rd birthday, and wee Jock was up that ladder and into the turret as nimbly as ever he did." They did two displays. The first was at a Memorial Service for the 484th Bombardment Group who flew B17 Flying Fortresses at their old airfield at Grafton Underwood. The second was to steam railway enthusiasts at Ripley, where steam enthusiasts of the Midland Railway Trust were holding a "Railways at War" weekend. Between Coningsby and Grafton Underwood, the Spitfire and the Hurricane did simulated rear attacks on the Lancaster - much to Wee Jock's delight.

Finally, they flew over Dunholme Lodge.

The airfield has long since been returned to farming, but they could all see in crop-marks the outline of buildings, hard-standings, perimeter tracks, and the runways. "For so many old friends," mused John, "those runways were their last contact with England."

Finally, they set course for Coningsby. John did not say who was piloting the Lancaster.

* For further reading see:
Martin Middlebrook, "The Nuremberg Raid", published by Allen Lane, 1973.

This is not the only example of a son following a father in flying the same type of aircraft - it has been done on Canberras - but it is unique for a Lancaster, and likely to remain so!

THE
REAR
GUNNER

Chapter 9

Another June day; another old folks bus; another tour round the hangar. A cheerful, kindly group of pensioners enjoying the sunshine and each other's company.

That's what they really come for, thought the Guide to himself, as the party strolled, shuffled, eased its way down the side of the hangar. It's the company, he thought; he wondered how many of the thirty or so in the party lived on their own; how many fought the spectre of loneliness, counting the days to the next Club Outing, or Bingo...

He talked to the party about the Spitfires - the fighter Marks, and the blue one - the photographic reconnaissance aircraft. Of course they had all lived through the battle, thought the Guide. But how many, he wondered, lived underneath it, saw the vapour trails, the patterns in the skies over southern England as young men fought for their lives.........

He talked to the party about the Hurricane and how it could absorb battle damage. He wondered whether any of the old folk now listening to him had themselves suffered - bore the scars of battle. And into his mind came those lines that he had had to learn at school:

......Then will he strip his sleeve and show his scars
And say, "These wounds I had on Crispin's Day........

Not now, they don't, he said to himself, as he lead the party on to the Lancaster. And - as Guides do - he talked about the rear turret and the men who occupied it. "The loneliest man in the aircraft," he heard himself saying...........

When the tour finished, one elderly man hung back.

"Can I go and touch the Lanc.?" he asked.

It's a question the Guides don't want - for it is laid down, sensibly enough - that the public do not touch the aircraft. But there was something about this man.....something about the eyes.......

"Well," said the Guide, "I can't authorise it, but I will have a word with someone who might."

And shortly after, the pensioner was escorted back to the Lancaster.

It was some weeks later that the Guide received a letter which he read; read again, and then sat in silent thought for a long time.

The letter is reproduced here in full, except that the name and address have been withheld - for reasons that become obvious. The writer has agreed to its publication - for it may help others whose scars have not yet healed.

5. 7. 93

Dear Sir,

This letter is going to begin with sincere apologies and end with profound thanks. I telephoned your Memorial Flight H.Q. a few weeks ago and through a process of elimination, the gentleman who answered was able to give me your name and address. I suppose the reference to Scone Flying school in Perth would be the final clue as to your identity.

I was a member of the Pensioners' Club from Nottinghamshire whom you showed round the Memorial Flight on Thursday 10 June, four weeks ago. In a form of complete desperation, I asked you would it be possible for me to touch the Lanc. It was a desperate plea and you answered it with the words "I will have a word." I still could not believe that recognition would be granted. I must now go back to the beginning of all my problems.

One evening nearly three years ago during the Gulf War, while watching a TV News Bulletin, they showed the U.S. bombers homing in on a target, the pictures coming from in-flight photography from the attacking plane. It was during these moments my mind literally blew up, and I started to sob uncontrollably. After about four hours, I was steadying up and my wife who held my hand throughout without fully understanding at the time what it was all about, made me take two of her sleeping tablets (one was normal). They did, eventually, get me to sleep.

What I could never understand and still cannot, was, and is, why after fifty years this had happened.

It was as if I had been in a cocoon all that time and suddenly I was thrown back into reality of those former days, or should I say nights.

To cut this short, after two years of sleepless, sometimes broken nights, I went to my G.P. I could not explain fully, without breaking down. (I was always bloody-minded, hence the delay in seeing the Doc.) My Doctor arranged for a Counsellor Psychiatrist to visit me at home, but from the first meeting we were never on the same wavelength, so that ended abruptly.

It was when I spoke to you that day last month, I knew we were on the same wavelength, and things started to go in the right direction mentally.

I cannot describe the feelings within me rationally

Lancaster - Rear Turret.

as I walked towards the Lanc. I know that did take courage of a sort.

But the feelings I got when I eventually touched the rear turret and put my forehead against it, were uplifting and consolatory. I walked away light-footed, light-hearted and (to coin a common term) a new man. I don't remember much of the coach run home, but from that night onwards I have slept the sleep of the Just, and back to a more normal and certainly of a more ameliorate self.

My apology at the beginning was for my delay in writing you, the one doubt remaining, could I still remain together when writing about it all. The answer is Yes, undoubtedly, and I am eternally indebted to you and exceedingly grateful for your term of Wisdom "I will have a word."

God bless you.   Yours sincerely,

ex-Rear Gunner.

F.I.D.O.

Chapter 10

"Not a good day for visitors!"

Some half dozen Guides at the Battle of Britain Memorial Flight at Coningsby lounged around their crew Room (actually a mobile hut kindly donated by an industrial firm in Lincoln) which served as office, Visitors' Reception, store room, information centre, rest room and Guides refreshment area. In the latter function, the lack of water supply, sink or drainage proved no bar to the production of tea and coffee - such was the ingenuity of former wartime Air Engineers and Bomb Aimers. Clutching their steaming mugs for warmth, they gazed gloomily out of the windows towards a Car Park totally hidden by a blanket of dense fog.

Memories of that enemy of all aviators - fog - returned to haunt them. "Proper Clampus Magnus", observed one motionless figure.

"D'you ever do a FIDO landing ?" asked Bob of no one in particular. "I remember one night at Ludford............"

F.I.D.O. - officially - Fog Intensive Dispersal Operation - was one of those Second World War inventions which today amaze those to whom it comes as news. It could have been conceived and executed only as a desperate wartime measure, yet as such it was little short of brilliant. Down each side of a runway ran perforated pipes; in dense fog situations which developed after Bomber Squadrons had departed and before their return, neat petrol was pumped along the pipes and ignited.. Thus two great lines of fire - visible through the fog

from a distance - lifted the fog from the immediate vicinity of the runway and enabled aircraft to land.. The cost in fuel was enormous (a standard FIDO system used up to 90,000 gallons of petrol per hour) - but this was entirely justified by the number of lives saved. The exact figure of Allied aircrew is not known but it can be estimated for 2524 aircraft landed safely through FIDO - probably in excess of 3,500 aircrew!

Before Bob had time to recount what happened at Ludford, another memory was stirred.

"I remember Jim doing a FIDO landing," the speaker chuckled, "and got a right bollocking......

"Go on, then.........."

"He was on 76 Squadron at Holme-on-Spalding-Moor. Flying Halifaxes; can't remember whether they were III's or V's - they had both. Anyway, Jim was flying his usual aircraft, U for Uncle, and.....what? when? oh, winter of '43/'44, probably early 44; the weather was awful. Now the Squadron had paid a rather tiring visit to the Fatherland when in rolled the fog. The first few 76 aircraft back managed to get in at Holme: Jim was unlucky - he had two go's on the Beam. First time he missed on the right; went round again and second time he missed on the left. Control said he missed the hangar as well, - but only just! Jim said he never saw it, in fact he couldn't see anything. So Control said he - and all those others in the queue - would have to divert to Kinloss.

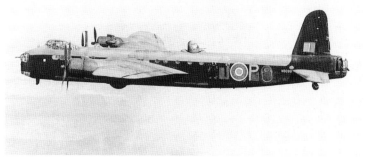

(Photograph Crown Copyright/MoD)

The four-engined Short Stirling.

Well, Jim had had a rough time and hadn't enough fuel to make Kinloss, so he was ordered to ditch off Hornsea."

The standard practice when an aircraft could not land due to fog and had insufficient fuel to reach the diversion airfield, was for the aircraft to be flown to a point on the coast when the crew would bale out; the aircraft set to fly out to sea and eventually come down when it ran out of fuel. It saved lives but was the waste of a perfectly good aircraft.

"Jim flew Uncle towards Hornsea. On the way, they saw a glow on the ground which turned out to be a FIDO installation (on test, though they were unaware of that.) Jim radioed back to Holme who said they could have a go at getting in. Uncle's crew did not know what airfield it was so they put out a Mayday and were given permission to land.

To land on FIDO for the first time was an unnerving experience. The terrific heat generated swallowed up oxygen and caused vicious downdraughts around the runway. This made for a very bumpy ride, especially on the final approach when it seemed that some great, unseen force was trying to drag you down. Once between the lines over the runway the heat caused the aircraft to float, and if your concentration lapsed for a moment to throw you violently and without warning to either side. The heat could be felt inside the aircraft, but the relief when you were finally down was indescribable.

"Jim, of course, had not done a FIDO landing before and remembering the warnings made a good approach; in fact he had touched down when Uncle swung smartly off the runway..........and went

straight through the piping! You see, this was an experimental installation and the pipes were fixed higher than normal. Jim's landing was the first time it had been used. The Halifax went through the piping and put the entire system out. Jim thought he would be commended for saving the aircraft; - instead he received a right royal bollocking for wrecking the system!"

There were chuckles all round at yet another incident which demonstrated the old adage - "There ain't no justice" - more so than ever among the crews of Bomber Command.

"What about Ludford then, Bob?"

"Could have been the same night," responded Bob. "February '44 this was. Lot of bad weather about that time. Well, Ludford, up on the Lincolnshire Wolds, was fitted out with FIDO, and on this particular night the whole County was fog-bound so not only did Ludford have its own aircraft........."

"Who was there then?"

"101 was based there, but they had aircraft from many other Stations queueing up to get in. Now this incident started when a four-engined Stirling with a new, young crew had been sent on a diversion raid - probably mine-laying - and had lost an engine through enemy action. They found their own airfield covered with fog; were diverted to Ludford, and requested a priority clearance on three engines. This was granted by the young WAAF controller, but

The twin-engined Vickers Wellington.

immediately a further emergency call was received in the tower. This was from a Wellington aircraft based at Leconfield in Yorkshire which was lost on a training flight, and the crafty Royal Canadian Air Force pilot demanded an even more urgent clearance as he had only two engines!"

(The Wellington was a twin-engined aircraft: the pilot didn't say he had lost engines - only that he had two, which was normal.)

"The WAAF controller, in the heat of the moment, granted him a 'straight-in' landing and told the Stirling to give way.

Down on the ground, aircraft were being 'parked' wherever there was space. When the Stirling eventually landed it was marshalled along the perimeter track and parked - next to the Wellington. When the lads emerged they saw the Canadians grouped round the Wellington's main wheels grinning cheerfully. When the light dawned the Stirling crew were furious and advanced through the murk telling the Canadians exactly what they thought of them and their mothers. Finally the Canadian pilot said they had a choice, 'Are you going to fight us, or shall we go to the nearest pub?'

You're right, they all landed up at the Black Horse in Ludford village. Now I heard about this incident from some of the 101 Squadron chaps, but the story was soon round the Station and the locality, for at 4.00am the next morning the Landlord of the Black Horse phoned the Ludford Guardroom and asked for the services of a lorry and several strong blokes. They loaded - none too gently - the comatose crews of two bomber aircraft into the back of the 4-ton Bedford and transported them back to the Station. Well, they'd made their first FIDO landings and survived; not a bad reason for getting drunk!"

Bob added that some of the former 101 Squadron chaps were still around, as is the Black Horse - though it's had several changes of Landlord since 1944.

"Who's for another cuppa?" asked Mick from the corner of the room.

There were grunts and other noises of assent.

"Right," said Mick holding up a large, clear and very empty plastic container. "Who's going for the water?"

No one moved or spoke.

"You're a right miserable lot of sods," Mick pattered over to the door.

"Can't see," said someone by the window, "....too damn foggy."

The door slammed behind Mick as he disappeared into the murk.

————————⊙————————

N.B.: Fl. Lt. F. W. Cole, DFC, (Jim in the story above) died on 5 May 1997.

ALL IN THE DAY'S WORK 3 - THE GROUND CREW

Chapter 11

From 1994 until retirement in 1996, the Engineering Officer for B.B.M.F. was Warrant Officer Len Sutton. Len is a local man from the neighbouring town of Horncastle and has spent a lifetime in the R.A.F. Working through his team of 21 Technicians, his brief at Coningsby was to keep the aircraft flying - no easy task given their age.

Whatever the source of spares, there is one basic rule which Engineers must follow - B.B.M.F. aircraft must be maintained to the same airworthiness standards that govern all R.A.F. aircraft. There are folders of rules, regulations, orders, procedures and schedules to help them and there is an annual audit to ensure that the Spitfires are as airworthy as the 5 and 29 Squadron Tornados with which they share the airfield. There are no concessions.

That basic rule destroys the popular notion that farmers' barns and old ladies' garages yield a wealth of useable bits and pieces. And the stories of new engines and airframes buried in their original crates at the end of the war? Len has heard them all but succinctly observes, "I have yet to see one unearthed," and adds with an engineer's logic, "and they've hardly been stored in conditions of correct temperature and humidity over the past 50 years".

And that is important - for all items particular to B.B.M.F., such as Lancaster tyres, are stored at Coningsby under exactly those conditions. All parts are binned, shelved, labelled and stacked with locations and quantities organised by computer. Thus if a display aircraft goes unserviceable at, say, Edinburgh, the right part can be despatched with the right Technician and the right tools for an overnight repair to be completed so that the aircraft can make the display time the following day.

Some spares such as nuts and bolts, switches and instruments, are available from normal R.A.F. stock. This also applies to radio equipment for all B.B.M.F. aircraft are fitted with modern VHF radio - essential for flying in today's busy airspace.

Len comments that his job became interesting when any part was not available from R.A.F. sources. With over 40 Spitfires; many Dakotas; a few but increasing number of Hurricanes, and many Mustangs with Merlin engines currently flying, there is an extensive world-wide industry supporting this growing number of historic aircraft. To enable him to purchase off the shelf from this network, the Engineer has a budget - but even in these circumstances Len had to ensure that the supplying organisation had been duly certified by the airworthiness authorities, and the origin of each spare shown on documentation.

The final option, when a part cannot be obtained from any source, is to have it made. Safety

Rolls Royce Merlin engine awaiting fitment to Lancaster.

(Photograph Courtesy of Len Sutton)

standards are again paramount; a genuine manufacturer's drawing, and the correct raw material specification must be provided, and the manufacturer duly certified. (B.B.M.F. holds all the original A. V. Roe Lancaster drawings on microfiche.) The Flight has many friends in industry, and Len can vouch for the enthusiasm of many managers to help. "We have had Dakota control cables made over the Christmas holidays; work put onto a night shift, and put on to overtime to produce a necessary item. In turn, the Flight always tries to give our friends in industry good publicity for their efforts."

Just occasionally, Len has been on a treasure hunt. Tipped off by an Engineering Officer in the West Midlands, Len visited a country estate where the affable owner led him to the upper floor of an old barn. Wishing he hadn't worn his best black shoes, Len saw amid the potato boxes, grain sacks, dust and cobwebs a number of perspex windows. There were four patterns, and six of each pattern, and had been bought by the owner's father at an auction to be used as cloches! Len brought back one set to Coningsby where they were identified as the sliding and hinged panels from the Wellington cockpit. All these parts, though no longer fit for use, are now with the Wellington Restoration Group at Weybridge, where they will be displayed.

B.B.M.F.'s Engineering Officer is much more than simply an engineer; he has to be able to turn his hand to other duties. One day, Len found two ladies wandering aimlessly outside the hangar: they turned out to be the Mayor of Lancaster and her daughter, the Mayoress. Having come to present some Certificates to the C. O., they had somehow lost their official escort, and into the breech stepped our Engineer. In fact, Len found them a charming couple - not like the lady in an official party whom Len showed round one weekend. He had said that Spitfire AB910 was the only aircraft in the Flight at that time painted in colours she had actually worn on D-day.

"Why do you call a Spitfire 'she?" the lady demanded with some force. Political correctness never being one of Len's weaknesses, he turned and looked again at AB910. She wore the markings of 402 Squadron with the black and white invasion stripes. (see photograph on Page 47)

"I think it has something to do with grace and beauty", replied Len. The lady, a good deal younger than the Spitfire, and not unattractive herself, nevertheless remained frosty for the rest of her time in the hangar.

One piece of information which always went down well with the ladies concerned the "purchase" during wartime of Spitfires by individuals or organisations. A donation of £5,000 to the Ministry of Aircraft Production meant your name or that of the organisation was painted on the side of the next Spitfire off the production line, or you could have such legends as 'Dog Fighter' or 'Flying Scotsman'. "But", said Len, "the one that always produced a laugh was the revelation that there really was a Spitfire named 'The National Federation of Hosiery Manufacturer's Association'."

Len wasn't in his engineer role either when he met a memorable couple; he was being a photographer. The Lancaster and two of the fighter aircraft had just returned from a display and were being marshalled ready to be brought into the hangar. It made an unusual photograph with wingtips and propellor blades all in shot and Len, concentrating on his viewfinder, was disturbed by a voice in his ear, "I used to fly in that, you know."
"Fly in what?"
"That Lanc. On 82 Squadron in Africa. Years ago." The Australian at his elbow grinned cheerfully. Len made an arrangement for him and his wife to visit

when the hangar was quiet, and together they boarded the Lancaster, climbed over the spars and into the cockpit. The Australian sat at the navigator's table and chuckled, "I used to sit here for up to twelve hours at a time." He had been an Army Sergeant surveyor flying with 82 Squadron when they carried out survey work in Africa, sometimes flying the breadth of the continent up at 30,000 feet. He and his wife were a charming couple and he was the only person whom Len met in two years who had actually flown in the Lancaster during its active Service career.

Len claims, however, that his most memorable visitor was a fourteen year old boy from Yorkshire, who wrote to Len asking for drawings and photographs of the instrument panels of the Lancaster as he was constructing a computerised simulator. This impressed both Len and the C. O., and while Len sent him copies of the requested drawings, he said that if he wanted photographs, he'd best come and take them himself. Within days his father brought him to Coningsby and Len says he was completely taken aback by this polite, knowledgeable and properly confident young man. After some two hours of chat, photography, and discussion with Sqdn. Ldr. Rick Groombridge about stick forces when flying the Lancaster, Len escorted them back to the car park. Finally, Len said, "You seem to be the sort of young man who has already ridden on the footplate of the Flying Scotsman."

Merlin engine installed in Lancaster. View from cockpit

"Oh, yes, I have," responded the fourteen year old. Len turned away, intent on keeping an eye on that young man's career.

Saturday 19 August 1995 was a special day for Len and his crew. It was - in one sense - like any other display day; it was also the 50th anniversary of VJ day. There were to be celebrations in the capital and B.B.M.F. had a highly visible and audible part to play - for the veterans on parade; the crowds who had gathered, and the millions who would be watching on television. The Lancaster was to drop poppies on the Mall; a Spitfire and Hurricane together with a Naval Firefly would lead the main fly-past, and at dusk, a lone Spitfire would fly up the Thames. A back-up Spitfire had to be held at Northolt; a second reserve back at Coningsby, and the Dakota despatched to Belfast for their Sunday celebrations.

That meant all the Flight's aircraft had to be ready to fly - an unusual circumstance in itself, but there was another, extra job for the ground crew - the loading of one million poppies into the Lancaster's bomb-bay.

This was the second poppy drop and the protective wire-mesh panels, which are fitted into the bomb-bay to protect the throttle and flying control cables from the poppies, had been kept from the first occasion and fitted earlier in the month.

With two weeks to go, Len telephoned the British Legion warehouse in Maidstone to arrange collection of the poppies.
"Why?" asked the Manager. "Haven't you got them?"
"No," replied Len "haven't **you** got them?"
"No," responded the Manager, "the Army collected them some time ago!"

Sod's Law was operating again. In the end it was a simple error: the Army had indeed collected them along with their own one million poppies which were to go on a Hercules freighter as a back-up to the Lancaster.

Having recovered the poppies, Sergeant Paul Blackah and his men set about loading the Lancaster. Decanting them from their boxes into black plastic bin-liners, the poppies were fed into the bomb-bay through an access panel in the bomb-aimer's compartment. Of course there were blockages to be cleared but eventually the Lancaster stood stuffed like a turkey. Because it is normal procedure to check the hydraulic pumps on start-up by opening the bomb doors, Len had Sgt Blackah wire-lock the bomb door selector handle closed, otherwise there might have been an embarrassing poppy drop at Coningsby prior to departure!

Len has the last word. "The weather that Saturday was kind to us. It was sunny, warm and with only a slight breeze from the west almost straight down the Mall. Paul had remembered his wire-cutters; the poppies arrived on target; the two fighters helped to lead the fly-past; the Dakota arrived in Belfast, and the oldest flying Spitfire, P7350 gently flew the Thames that evening. The spare aircraft weren't needed.

"Two remarks I particularly remember. After the Lancaster had taxied in, Mike Chatterton said to me, 'It was most strange watching myself flying down the Mall on that big TV screen in Green Park.' The following morning after Alan Martin had brought P7350 home, he said of his flight up the Thames at dusk, 'You know, that was the finest display I've ever done'.

"I remember walking round the hangar that Saturday evening in the quiet when the aircraft had been put to bed and the doors locked. There was the odd poppy lying under the Lancaster, and AB 910, the Mark V Spitfire, although polished and ready for flight hadn't moved all day and had missed all the excitement."

THE
WEDDING

Chapter 12

Spitfire AB910 starting up. Douglas would probably have been flying a Spitfire of this

Ask most strangers for their image of Lincolnshire and they will say 'remote' or perhaps 'fenland' - thinking of the bulbfields around Spalding. In fact, the most prominent geological feature is the ridge of Limestone which runs from the Humber Estuary, through Lincoln, to the Leicestershire border. On this ridge were sited some of the earliest airfields in the country; the RNAS had built an airship base at Cranwell by 1917, and the RAF College was established there by 1920. In World War II Lincolnshire was host to forty-five RAF airfields - more than any other single county.

It is hardly surprising therefore that many former members of the RAF visit this county, for apart from present airfields there are places where Service history abounds - the museum at Cranwell; the Lincs Aviation Museum on the site of the former airfield at East Kirkby, and the Battle of Britain Memorial Flight at Coningsby.

Many of these visitors have stories to tell; often the most interesting are eventually told by those most reluctant to talk. Modesty is not always the restraining factor: for some the memories are too painful; others feel their past experiences are no longer relevant, not worth telling. For one recent visitor, however, the past has become the present.

Most Lincolnshire-based personnel were part of

Bomber Command; Douglas was not. In 1943 he was flying Spitfires, and on one operation his Squadron had been 'bounced' by enemy fighters whilst on escort duties over occupied France. In the ensuing melee, Douglas had become separated from the rest of his Squadron. While making his way back across the Channel, he spotted a lone Dornier Bomber, its port engine trailing thick smoke, limping towards the safety of the Continent. Right, thought Douglas, I'll finish this fellow off ..... make sure he doesn't make landfall. The position was favourable: he was up-sun of the German and unlikely to have been spotted. Wait till he's beneath, then wing-over and down ..... tuck in behind him.

At which point Douglas had to throttle back for he was gaining much too fast on the crippled bomber. A thin wisp of smoke was now coming from its over-heated starboard engine; it was steering erratically as if its pilot was having difficulty controlling direction, and it was losing height rapidly.

He must have seen me by now thought Douglas but the rear gunner made no attempt to bring his guns to bear. They pointedly obstinately upwards as if the gunner had collapsed over the breeches, depressing them and tipping the barrels up towards a diving phantom enemy. It was eerie: like a Marie Celeste of the skies, unseeing, unknowing, except that this ship was not going to stay afloat much longer!

He was far too close.

Why had he not fired and downed the thing? Why had he allowed himself to be drawn into this dangerous situation? Douglas could not explain. He drew level with the Dornier, perhaps some fifty feet away, concentrating on the cockpit. He could see the German pilot quite clearly in the bright air and then the row of torn holes that racked the fuselage and cockpit. Deliberately it seemed, the German turned his head and looked at the Spitfire. Then as if in salute, he raised his right hand. Douglas could see the thumb and one, perhaps two fingers; the rest of the hand was missing, the leather of his sleeve and shoulder dark-stained. As if mesmerised, Douglas returned the gesture.

Then the Dornier lurched and dropped; Douglas broke out of his reverie and, looking down, realised with horror that he had re-crossed the French coast. Full throttle, and he turned for home with not another thought for the Dornier until after he had landed safely at base.

Douglas survived. The ensuing peace was no easier

for him than for many who had had their young lives interrupted by five years of war. Despite the austerity and privation of the post-war years, Douglas survived and prospered. In the fullness of time he married and raised a family. The years passed and in turn he became a grandfather. Son had followed father into the Royal Air Force, and by the early/mid 80's his son had been posted to Germany.

Visits abroad to his grandchildren were a source of rare delight to Douglas. Now retired, he could indulge teenage Christopher and 11-year old Karen: despite the warnings and sotto voce mutterings of daughter-in-law, he spoiled them with unashamed indulgence and they loved him for it, and, yes, they were proud of him, too.

It was on one of those holidays that the children persuaded Grandad to visit a cafe much frequented by the younger set. Karen and Chris seemed to be well-known there and it was the proprietor who took their order. Karen's pride bubbled over, "This is my Grandad - he was a fighter pilot with the RAF during the War!"

"Was he now! Well, we had our Luftwaffe pilots too, you know. Do you think he would like to meet one? He speaks English." The proprietor nodded towards a group on the other side of the restaurant - pretty much like any other family group, noisy,

Spitfire AB910. This aircraft made three sorties over the beaches of Normandy on D-Day and is shown in the markings she had on that day.

mostly cheerful, lively and enjoying themselves. He moved over to the elderly man in the group and whispered in his ear. Probably in his mid-70's, short, thick-set, his thinning hair brushed straight back, he looked across at the little English party and without hesitation, rose and crossed the room. This was rather more than Douglas had bargained for, but he stood, shuffled round an adjoining table and, looking the former Luftwaffe man in the eye, he grasped and shook the proffered hand.

Great God almighty!

He couldn't help it. Bad manners it might be to examine another's disability but Douglas just had to look down at the hand he had just shaken: thumb, forefinger, half the middle finger - the rest missing. The German laughed: "One of your RAF friends did that to me, but don't be embarrassed; within a few minutes another RAF pilot saved my life. But come, meet my family. Bring your little friends - your Grandchildren? Come and sit with us, won't you?"

Two hours later, the two elderly men were still there, heads close together over their Pils.

And that was almost the end of Douglas' story. One of the listeners asked him if he had continued to see his former adversary after that first re-union. "Oh, yes," he said, "many times. We all became great friends over the years. In fact, I was in Germany three weeks ago, at the wedding. You see, my grandson has just married his grand-daughter. If my wife was here, she'd show you the photographs."

———————⊙———————

"The Wedding" was first published on its own in a privately circulated Journal in the autumn of 1995 where it was seen by Tom. In a letter of 26 November 1995, Tom wrote, "As soon as I had read it, I filed it under 'Sermons' since I knew I was due to preach at the annual Remembrance Sunday Service which took place earlier this month. After the Service, many of those present told me how much they had enjoyed the story which I had used as an illustration in an address on the theme of 'Building Peace'.

THE PARABLE OF THE LEAVEN

Chapter 13

Ask Tom what has been the most important element in his life and he will answer unhesitatingly, 'The Parable of the Leaven'.* That is not an answer which would enlighten many people for the Leaven is hardly the best known of the Parables. Nor is Tom's story well-known - more's the pity - for it deserves to be. It is the story of a man who has taken that parable and acted it out with his own life.

Tom regards himself as very lucky. A Church attender in his youth, he regards having a Curate allergic to Sunday School kids as lucky for it gave him the chance to teach, and even become Superintendent for a year. Being the eldest in a family of four, he sat in silence and set a good example as tea was arranged to coincide with Children's Hour on the wireless. Thus he was lucky enough to hear every Friday Commander Stephen King-Hall and learnt about the outside world - from the breakdown of the Disarmament Conference, through the American-Japanese Naval talks and Munich, right up to the outbreak of World War II. Thus he regarded himself as politically aware when he went up to the University of Birmingham to read Engineering.

Tom joined the Royal Air Force in 1941; because of his technical expertise he was trained as a radar operator and wore the coveted Brevet RO, very rare and so secret that all who wore it were not permitted to say what the letters meant! This situation was so ridiculous that after a few months the Brevet was withdrawn and replaced with N for Navigator.

By January 1942, Tom was with 153 (a Night-fighter Squadron); in July of that year he transferred with his New Zealand pilot to 488 Squadron where they spent their time chasing German weather aircraft and becoming numb with actionless patrols.

In January 1943, Tom was moved to a Special Duties Squadron and life became more interesting. In low-flying Wellingtons, Tom and his crew were finding out about German radar, on the ground, on ships and submarines, and airborne equipment.

On 26 May 1943, Tom's aircraft was shot down. Despite the Wellington being ablaze the entire crew baled out and all except Tom landed in the sea. Tom remembers little about the descent: he was unconscious. Because of operational requirements he had not gone through the normal Operational Training Unit but instead had been sent to a squadron which was converting from Defiants to Beaufighters to pick up a pilot and train with him on the squadron. Consequently, no-one had told him to remove his oxygen mask before baling out. This mask projected forward from the face, and the parachute - released from its chest harness - nipped smartly upwards and collided with the mask, forcing the head back and usually breaking the neck. Tom was made of sterner stuff: he was just out for the count.

* He told them also this parable: 'The Kingdom of Heaven is like yeast which a woman took and mixed with half a hundredweight of flour till it was all leavened.' Matthew 13.33

'Be on your guard, I said, against the leaven of the Pharisees and Sadducees.' Matthew 16.11

To say he landed on dry land would be metaphorical, True it was Dutch soil but it was also a drainage channel. Very damp; very muddled and confused, Tom dragged himself up the bank, rolled up his parachute to hide it, (aircrew were advised to bury parachutes if possible, not easy in Dutch pastures) and put it under a tree. He wandered from the ditch to a nearby road, and recalls trying to find the emergency compass which all aircrew carried for such a contingency.

He was picked up by a group of Dutch workers who had to cross the road at that point to reach the dairy where they were employed. There a Dutchman, who spoke some English, warned him of the search by the Germans for the crew of the aircraft which had been seen to come down in the sea, and added that they would all be shot if they gave him assistance. With Tom's agreement, he was handed over and thus began his two-year stretch as a prisoner of war.

The main camp for captured airmen was Stalag Luft III at Sagan in Poland, manned by Luftwaffe personnel who jealously maintained their right to guard their own kind. Of course there were attempts at escape; this was the duty of captured aircrew, but the odds were high and stacked heavily against the would-be escapers. The Guards knew that such attempts would be made and a constant cat-and-mouse relationship existed.

Prisoners had to make the most of the situation and cope as best they could with restriction and confinement and living on top of each other. Above all, they had to accept the loss of their personal freedom for an unknown length of time. Tom learnt German, and having something of a facility for languages taught it to others. He also played in the camp orchestra. He was involved in escape attempts; not his own, but when an attempt was officially approved by the Escape Committee various talents were recruited as required. Thus it was that Tom became a part of one of the most famous escape stories of the Second World War - the Wooden Horse.*

He vaulted over that horse; and vaulted and went on vaulting as long as it took for the two below ground to dig their way forward; fill the leg-bags with sand, and climb up into the body of the horse when it would be carried away to safety.

As with all the other vaulters, Tom carried away the sand in the leg-bags concealed within his trouser-legs and dispersed it under the huts they lived in, mixing the bright yellow sand from underground with the grey sand already there.

But it was as the violinist that he came into his own. With time running short, another escaper joined the original two and the dispersal of the

*The story is told in Eric Williams' book, "The Wooden Horse" published by Collins, 1958.

sand became a major problem. Under a floor it had to go; the barber's shop was chosen, and while the dispersal was in progress Tom played his violin at an open window. Signals were agreed, and on the approach of a guard Tom turned his solo into a choir practice - all the men in the hut crowded round and sang lustily. For a month, they kept up this charade; it needed cool heads and strong nerves to enable - finally - three men to make their successful bid for freedom.

The escape was discovered some two and a half hours after the three officers surfaced beyond the wire and made their dash into the cover of the woods. A German guard, coming on duty, fell - literally - into the tunnel exit. Now there were very few prisoners in the camp who knew that anyone had escaped; security had to be tight, and only those actively involved were privy to the plans.

By lights out at 11pm., all prisoners were in their bunks. Suddenly there was a commotion: the hut doors were being unlocked and thrown open. There was shouting, "Stay in your rooms!" Guards were stamping about, taking up positions in the corridor and outside the huts, their Alsatians

barking. Eventually the light was switched on and the Photographic guards came into the room with their boxes of Identity Cards bearing details and photographs of each prisoner. They went from bunk to bunk, checked everyone, switched off the light and left. The doors were again locked.

Tom found sleep difficult. His thoughts were with the three escapers: 'Have they caught them? or shot them? Only three hours start, even if they're still free! They'd hoped for the whole night.'

Tom was glad to get up early: he was the breakfast stooge and went to collect boiling water and whatever news he could glean. The Germans had first to discover how many had got away, and then the identities of the escapers in order to issue descriptions. Tom learnt that Huts 62 to 67 had been checked, but Wing Commander Collard had found some means of short-circuiting the mains and blowing the fuses before Huts 68 and 69 could be checked. So from the previous night the guards knew that three were missing from Hut 62 but not if there were any others missing. Tom passed this news on to his room-mates; they lay and wondered what would happen next.

Checking the identities of the entire East Camp (approaching some 1,500 men) was a lengthy and tedious business. It frayed the nerves and raised the tempers of those whose job it was to keep the checked men separate from those who weren't.

Roll-call was at 08.00 hrs. They were formed up in a hollow rectangle, Huts 62 and 63 on one side, Huts 64 to 67 with their backs to the barbed wire fence, with Huts 68 and 69 forming the third limb facing Huts 62 and 63. The counting took its normal slow course with Sergeant Stuhlmeyer pacing along the front rank with his Corporal behind the rear rank checking each file of five. Eventually, with the 'Sick in Quarters' added in, the Sergeant reported to the Major in charge of the parade. Twenty minutes later, the Photographic guards arrived and after lengthy and animated debate decided to start on the identities of Huts 68 and 69 which had not been checked the night before.

Meanwhile the rest of the prisoners remained good-humoured: after all, it was their day. Never before had an escape via a tunnel proved successful at Stalag Luft III, built to be impregnable as it was. This was another triumph for the Royal Air Force over the Luftwaffe - that was, provided Bill, Mike and Ollie were still at liberty. But this was 30 October on the Polish Border; it was a cold morning and most of the prisoners were scantily clad. They were hopping about, stamping and waving their arms to keep warm. One of the Army lads, who paraded separately at the end of each block of officers, was carrying a football. He willingly lent it to the RAF who started kicking it to and fro along the long lines. Of course the inevitable happened: someone booted it too hard, a rebound and out it shot, escaping onto the parade ground.

Tom darted out to retrieve it, but the Major spotted it, decided that this behaviour could not be tolerated and shouted to one of the guards, in English, the immortal command, "Arrest zat ball!"

The guard, encumbered by his long grey greatcoat and carrying his rifle and fixed bayonet in the 'Slope Arms' position, slowly approached the ball which lay at Tom's feet. At that moment, another prisoner appeared behind the guard and gestured for the ball. Tom kicked it over the guard's head; he turned and approached the prisoner who now had the ball. Soon others called for the ball which sped hither and thither with the guard's attempt to gain possession weakening all the time. By now the whole parade was enjoying the show, laughing and cheering.

This drove the Major to distraction.

Pink in the face, he bellowed for silence, which only caused greater laughter and merriment.

In the middle of all this confusion, Wing

Commander Collard, whose identity had already been checked, strolled quietly through the cordon of guards who did nothing to stop him, and up to Wing Commander Roger Maw, standing in front of Block 64. "I bet you your chaps can't score a try behind our lines!" he called out loudly.

"I bet you we can! " Wings Maw replied at the top of his voice and gestured to his men to attack. As one man they all surged forward, passing the soccer ball from one to another as in any textbook rugger attack. At the same time the Hut 68 men rushed to meet them regardless of whether they were carrying the ball or not. Any right-minded referee would have stopped the match, whilst the Germans would have been within their right to open fire, for the identity check had been foiled once again with those already checked irretrievably mixed up with those unchecked.

It was all too much for the elderly Major. He abandoned the check and ordered the guards to their quarters while he reported to the Kommandant, who in turn, sent for the compound's Senior British officer, Group Captain Kellett, and complained bitterly about the indiscipline of the British Officers.

Later that day Luftwaffe troops en masse sorted it out, but what might be judged as juvenile antics had gained an extra day for the escapers to reach the Baltic port of Stettin without their descriptions being broadcast to all. Those remaining in East Camp of Stalag Luft III were punished for their indiscipline: There were three Roll-calls each day thereafter; Red Cross Food parcels remained undistributed, and prisoners were locked in their huts by 5.00 pm each day: but Bill, Mike and Ollie made it back to England.

Stalag Luft III at the end of the war held some 10,000 'British' and American Air Force Officers. Certainly by then the Americans outnumbered the RAF, Dominions A.F. and European A.F. Officers. (The latter were given British citizenship so that they could be protected by the Swiss under the Geneva Convention.) All this came about partly because American aircraft had numerically larger crews but mainly because a higher proportion of airman shot down in daylight survived than those shot down at night. Tom comments, "When I was shot down, the survival rate was reckoned at one in ten. There was another personal motivation: I felt very deeply that I had to pull my weight on behalf of the other nine."

The prisoners in Stalag Luft III were not liberated there in Poland, however, but were marched westwards, in most cases in quite horrific conditions. They were intended to be hostages during the Fuhrer's last stand at Berchtesgarten. Tom was nearly there when liberated on 29 April - about the time that Hitler decided the game wasn't worth the candle. The SS troopers melted away seeking their own hide-outs, although not averse to firing a burst or two at P.O.W.'s as they fled. Once more, Tom considered himself one of the lucky ones. He was repatriated by the Americans to Reims where he was back with the Royal Air Force. After a ten day delay, he was finally flown back to the U.K. sitting on the floor of a Lancaster bomber.

Back in civilian life Tom became a student again, this time at the University of Cambridge where he read German and Russian, and was one of the founders of the United Nations Association in that university. A post teaching at the Royal Liberty School in Romford followed, and Tom began passing on his skills and knowledge to a younger generation; the process of the Leaven had begun.

In July 1948, Tom was on a vacation course at Marburg University in the American zone of Germany: he was in fact one of the first civilians allowed into occupied territory. Tom spent his evenings working in the American Library in the town. There was a course on International Affairs about to start in West Berlin; it had been organised by a group of American Quakers "...to effect reconciliation in Europe and build the bulwarks of peace..." and it was proposed to offer two places on the course to every European country.

At the time when this decision was taken, no American students had been invited. Because of the expense of ferrying them over the Atlantic, it was decided to choose from those already studying in Europe, and accordingly the American officers controlling the German universities in the American Zone were asked to nominate students for selection. The officer in charge of the University of Marburg was a woman and she refused to nominate a male American. (She was unimpressed by their preference for following Fraulein into the forest rather than attending lectures!) Instead, she nominated Tom, who although already deeply committed, was not told at that time that he would find himself acting as chief translator.

Of course, Tom went - though not quite in the way that everyone expected. Between the proposal and the event the Russians closed the Border posts into the Allied Sectors of the city, and so began what became known as the Berlin Airlift.

The delegates were flown in; the Course went on. The structure was that half the time was spent in lectures; the other half on a work camp. Together they succeeded in building a children's playground and had the satisfaction of seeing it used by German war orphans.

The lectures were in German, and those who delivered them of high calibre. Tom remembers one journalist, a specialist in German philosophy, who had survived a Concentration Camp, and it was he - with many others - who developed the theory behind this and subsequent International Conferences.

It went something like this: after 1918 it was thought that the way to ensure European peace was to keep Germany starved of all materials which could contribute to another war situation. Clearly, this had not worked; this time a different approach was required. If only the Gospel of Peace could be firmly implanted in the minds of a few individuals, carefully selected out of every one of the former warring nations, perhaps it could spread from them sufficiently throughout their nations that a climate of peace and understanding could be established - in the same way as yeast permeated the dough in Christ's Parable of the Leaven.

For Tom, this experience was more than political or international - it became very personal, for he met Gabriele, a German girl, whom he married back in England in July 1950. Together they set about making the dream a reality.

On the continent, there had been a setback. The Four Powers failed to agree on the value of currency so West and East went their separate ways with all the suspicion and distrust which became known as the Cold War. Back in Romford, Tom continued his teaching career, and he and Gabriele ran the U.N. Association Youth Forum. It is some measure of Tom's capabilities that in 1956 he was appointed Headmaster of a Warwickshire Grammar School which under his leadership became a large and hugely popular Comprehensive School. Tom held that post until his retirement in 1985. He has been a Lay Reader for many years, and worked for the Diocesan Readers Board and Christian Aid.

Did he not use the Russian he had so painfully learnt? (It is an extremely difficult language.) Twice he took 55-seater coaches full of Russian-speaking pupils from his school to Moscow, and once to Kiev. Here they were actually permitted to live in an Ukranian Pioneer Camp with Soviet members of this organisation. Tom sat on the Committee which worked out all the conditions for the exchange of teachers between British and Soviet schools. The leaven was at work in eastern Europe as well.

Does he play the violin now? Well, yes, music is still a hobby. Has he any other hobbies? A frown crosses his face, but he doesn't say, 'Do you really think I have time for hobbies?' - which he might well have done. Then, as if remembering something he had taken for granted, he admits to reading the Gospels. Don't we all at some time? Yes, but not in the original Greek - which language Tom has taught himself.

The engineer who wore his RO Brevet with pride has come a long way: the leaven has not stopped working yet.

18,000 FEET
WITHOUT A PARACHUTE

Chapter 14

Peter is a Guide with a definite sense of humour; an asset appreciated by those whom he escorts round the exhibits at the Battle of Britain Memorial Flight, and valued by his colleagues at all times. It is a quality which stood him in good stead after one incident which caused him to be the recipient of much good-natured banter.

It was an ordinary day, and an ordinary party whom Peter showed round the hangar. Yes, Spitfires and Hurricanes were fighter aircraft, but the Lancaster was - for Peter - the real aeroplane: that is not surprising given Peter's experience as a Bomb-Aimer who completed a tour of operations on a Lancaster Squadron.

And he talked, not just about the aircraft itself, but about the seven men who made up her crew - their positions and the jobs they did. How they were a team who supported each other; depended on each other's expertise to ensure the job they were set to do was well done. The coldest and loneliest place in the aircraft was that of the Rear-Gunner located between the two tall fins and rudders: it was his task to recognise that patch of dark in the darkness that was an enemy fighter - preferably before it saw the Lancaster - and do something about it. It was not an enviable job, and Peter made sure his parties heard all about the man popularly known as 'Tail End Charlie'

In his party on this particular day was a nine-year old boy who asked the question, "How did the Rear Gunner get out of his turret if the crew had to bale out?"

Peter explained that if it were possible, the gunner centralised the turret, opened the swing doors which lead back into the fuselage and reached for his parachute which was kept in a metal container on the other side of the doors. He clipped the 'chute onto the hooks of his harness and left by the side hatch.

If it were not possible to leave by the side hatch, the gunner could - having retrieved his parachute - turn the turret to the sideways or beam position by hand control, open the doors, and simply fall out backwards.

"Hope he remembered to take the parachute," said the boy.

"Didn't always happen......." responded Peter, and he told them about Flight Sergeant Nicholas Alkemade.

It is not known how many men have jumped 'chuteless and survived, but there are six documented cases of which Alkemade's is the best known. He was a Rear Gunner in 115 Squadron, and on 23 March 1944 was on his fifteenth

Peter with four other members of his Lancaster crew at R.A.F. Upwood, No 156 Squadron. May 1944. Peter is standing, left hand side.

Operation returning from a raid on Berlin when the Lancaster was caught by a German night-fighter and set on fire. Alkemade saw flames pouring back past his turret and heard the pilot give the 'Bale out!' order.

The small boy pricked up his ears: this was exciting stuff.

Peter continued with the story. Alkemade opened the doors for his parachute but it was too late; the fuselage was ablaze and his hands and wrists were scorched in the time it took to see his parachute pack burning in its stowage. Quickly, he slid back into his turret and closed the doors. He was faced with a choice: jump out to certain death, or stay put and fry. His mind was made up for him when the turret hydraulic lines caught fire and the flames spread to his clothing. Better to die cleanly, he thought: rotated the turret, and dropped into the night.

It was about midnight when the Lancaster was attacked at about 18,000ft: at about 3.00am Alkemade regained consciousness, lying on his back in snow in a pine forest. He was severely bruised; had numerous small cuts and scratches, and of course, the burns from the aircraft fire - otherwise he was uninjured. It was a miracle.

He slipped off his harness and left it in the snow. He tried to walk but gave that up as too painful and attracted attention by blowing his whistle. Eventually he was taken to hospital where he was treated - before his interrogation began.

Amongst other questions, the Gestapo wanted to know where Alkemade had hidden his parachute and laughed - accusing him of being a spy - when he said he had come down without one. It was only when the Germans found his discarded harness with the lift webs (which extend when the 'chute opens) still clipped down, that they were persuaded to investigate further. In the wreckage of the Lancaster, found some miles away, were discovered the metal remains of Alkemade's parachute; the ripcord handle and cable were found still in the stowage compartment.

So impressed were the German authorities that they issued a Certificate which corroborated Flight Sergeant Alkemade's claim to have dropped 18,000 ft without a parachute and to have survived without serious injury.

With this true story, Peter ended his tour of the hangar: one small boy left deeply impressed.

Later, at school, he was asked to write about his visit to the Battle of Britain Memorial Flight. What he wrote so tickled his parents that they sent a copy to the Guide-in-Charge. He in turn pinned it to the noticeboard, and this is what Peter's colleagues read :

"What I liked best at Coningsby was the Lancaster with it's long wings and it's big engine. I liked the Chipmunk as well. We had a Guide, he was called Mr Bond and he told us about the planes and who piloted them. Mr Bond was a bomb aimer in a Lancaster and at one time he jumped 17,000 feet and was caught by the Germans. They thought he was a spy. He had a broken coller bone and one arm and two broken legs. He escaped about thirteen years later and got a job at Coningsby.

Lee."

Perhaps not unnaturally, Peter took much flak from his fellow Guides and the school essay inspired the cartoon by the Late Derrick Clarey, reproduced here by kind permission of Mrs Stella Clarey.

Peter is still asked occasionally if he has his parachute with him !

Note:

The full story of Flight Sergeant Alkemade can be found in Chapter XV of Ian Mackersey's book, "Into the Silk" first published by Robert Hale in 1956; reprinted Mayflower 1978.

Peter, as drawn by fellow Guide Derrick Clarey, after telling a small boy the story of Fl. Sgt. Alkemade.

ALL IN THE DAYS WORK 4 - THE AIRCREW

Chapter 15

Fifty years ago, these aircraft of Battle of Britain Memorial Flight and thousands of others like them, were flown and crewed by men who were really accountants, farmers, teachers, engineers; or who had been simply schoolboys a year or so earlier. They accepted this translation as aviators as a job to be done and when it was all over, most went back into civilian life probably wiser and more mature individuals. What of the men who fly the aircraft today?

They are highly-trained, experienced, professional airmen, whose primary task is flying and teaching others to fly the Tornado; and for whom flying the aircraft of B.B.M.F. is a secondary duty. They must be prepared to give up virtually every weekend in the display season - and other free time to keep in constant practice.

Flying Second World War aircraft with piston engines and a tailwheel is a very different matter from the current Tornado with its massive twin jet engines; a mass of electronic gear, and a nose wheel. Until recently, pilots for the Lancaster were drawn from former Shackleton crews. Now the Shackleton is no longer in service, other sources are required.

The first former fighter pilot to command B.B.M.F. and pilot the Lancaster is Squadron Leader Rick Groombridge. He cut his teeth on Lightnings, Meteors and Vampires; flew with a Tornado squadron in the Gulf War, and was until recently an examiner of flying instructors on the Tornado.

As with all aircraft conversions in the Royal Air Force there is a training course which must be completed satisfactorily. Rick Groombridge makes clear that there are important limitations in flying B.B.M.F.'s aircraft, particularly with regard to weather conditions; wind strength and direction; and as the piston engine behaves differently from the jet, and the technique of taking-off and landing tail-wheel aircraft is different from those with a nose-wheel, it is back to basics on the Conversion course. Pilots being trained to fly piston-engined aircraft start by flying twenty five hours on the Chipmunk (a basic trainer of the Fifties and Sixties) at Coningsby. This is followed by a short but difficult course on the Harvard at Boscombe Down, then back to the Hurricane at Coningsby. Even then, things can go wildly wrong.

Rick Groombridge tells how things went wrong for a new fighter-pilot recruit, Flight Lieutenant Paul Shenton. "Paul had completed his 25 hour Chippie course and was cleared with a reasonable weather forecast to fly in the Chippie to Boscombe Down for the Harvard stage. Now I was at Lyneham that day with the Dakota making friends with the 1st Battalion, the Parachute Regiment for a rehearsal before dropping them out of the Dakota on the fiftieth anniversary of Arnhem.

In 1993 the Dakota joined the Flight, shown here flying over Lincoln Cathedral.

We were aware that the weather was deteriorating with increasing wind velocity and wondering about the viability of our own flight when, sitting in the Dakota, we heard on the radio that a Chipmunk was in the circuit. Now there aren't all that many Chippies in the Service and we guessed that this might be Paul.

So we jumped in the transport and rushed over to the Tower. The wind was increasing all the time; it was across the runway at Boscombe and out of limits for the Chippie. So Paul, short of fuel through headwinds, sensibly elected to land at Lyneham.

Unfortunately, by this time, the windspeed - although straight down the runway - was higher than the stalling speed of the aircraft!

'Has the Chipmunk landed?' we asked.

'Yes,' they replied, 'but he's still sitting on the runway.'

Rick guessed correctly that because of the wind creating a weathercock effect on the little Chipmunk, Paul was simply unable to turn off the runway so he collected the six heaviest men of his crew and drove out to where Paul sat with brakes hard on and the engine ticking over.

"I sat two guys on the starboard wing," Rick continued, "two on the port, and the other two on the tail. By this time a regular gale was blowing, and after congratulating Paul on getting the Chippie down at all, I climbed in the second seat - and very - gingerly, using brakes only, took twenty - five minutes to taxi the aircraft into safety. Not a bad introduction for a young pilot on the hazards of flying B.B.M.F. aircraft!"

Even if the weather is kind and the aircraft behaving perfectly, things can still go wrong. Hotels are a minefield for the unwary, and also apparently for Squadron Leader Groombridge. "In 1988, I was still a learner as far as the Lancaster was concerned. I was only the co-pilot when we were to display at the Wirral Airshow. We arrived on the Saturday prior to the display on the Sunday, and were taken direct to the Liverpool Moat House hotel at Toxteth. For some time we stayed in the foyer, in flying kit, distributing and signing brochures - spot of the P.R. stuff really - when in walked Cilla Black. She was very friendly; we got on well, and she mentioned that there was to be a big party in the hotel that night. It was to follow John Parrot's wedding; all the big snooker stars were to be there - Steve Davis and friends - and though we couldn't go to the dinner it was suggested that we would be welcome at the party afterwards.

We changed into civvies; walked up the hill for a meal, and then back to the Moat House and joined the party about 11.00pm. This was enjoyed by all of us, though you have to be careful with alcohol if you're flying next day. We retired to bed about a couple of hours later, and I was not best pleased to wake - I suppose it must have been something after three in the morning - and find I needed to pay a call.

Now it's a funny thing about hotels - if, like us - you seem to spend most weekends in them. They seem, particularly the bedrooms, to be built on a pattern. There's always the door to the bathroom on the right; on the left is the wardrobe door - that sort of thing. Anyway, on this occasion, I blundered through the bathroom door and found myself, by mistake, in the corridor. Before I could turn round the door had

slammed shut and locked behind me. And in the summer, I do not wear clothes in bed!

We do all sorts of training in the Air Force. We are regularly dumped in the North Sea to practice dinghy drill and rescue; we are carefully prepared should we come down in enemy territory; we know exactly what to do if an engine flames out, but I couldn't recall ever being left naked in a hotel corridor in the early hours of the morning and told to take appropriate action. Back to basic initiative training.

Just down the corridor was a trolley with the remains of someone's dinner. There were two unused napkins, and with these clutched fore and aft amidships I entered the lift and pressed for Ground Floor. You see, I thought at that time of the morning the foyer would be deserted and I could get a master key from the Night Porter. Well, that's a reasonable assumption, surely?

How could I know that the lift opened directly into the foyer, and that John Parrot's Party was just breaking up at the moment when the lift doors opened? Reception was packed, and all those jolly people were treated to the sight of this naked fellow with his napkin. Luckily I managed to get the doors shut again and was back outside my bedroom - still with an unsolved problem!

I had to take a chance. I'd not taken note of where

the rest of the crews' rooms were, but I knocked long on the door next to mine and to my relief it was eventually opened by my Boss. Despite his grudging agreement, I have often wondered what he really thought of being woken in the middle of the night by his co-pilot, naked apart from a napkin, asking to use his loo and spend the rest of the night on his bedroom floor! "

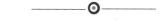

Problems with which the aircrew have to cope can arise from the most unexpected sources. Squadron Leader Groombridge was still co-pilot of the Lancaster when B.B.M.F. received an unusual request. "This was in 1986, I think. We were to display at Northolt on the Saturday and then do a fly-past over a formal Station Parade on the Sunday morning. We also had been asked to drop over the main runway the ashes of a former Officer who had served with distinction at Northolt.

We flew down on the Friday night. The ashes were left in a cardboard container overnight in the aircraft - which was parked in the open. Now the Lancaster leaks like a sieve and there was heavy overnight rain, so you can imagine the state of the cardboard and its contents - which just happened to be in a vulnerable spot. So, in an attempt to put matters right, the remains of the distinguished senior officer spent the next day on the radiator in the Boss's bedroom.

Unfortunately, we overdid it. By the Sunday morning, the box and its contents had set to a rock-like consistency. Rather than risk a minor explosion on the runway, the Lancaster was flown slightly to one side and the ashes dropped with dignity and unerring accuracy on the grass away from the Parade ground!"

The years 1990 to 1995 were crowded with Fiftieth Anniversaries, in commemoration of which the Memorial Flight played a full part. In 1995 there was the anniversary of Operation Manna and the Liberation of Holland. Over went the Lancaster - for it was from Lancaster aircraft that the food was dropped prior to the Liberation - together with two Spitfires. There was a monster fly-past over all the Manna drop areas - many of the aircraft participating were of Second World War vintage - the Catalina; the B17 from Duxford, the Sally B; and even Dutch aircraft which had been restored to flying condition.

Squadron Leader Groombridge was by this time the Commanding Officer of B.B.M.F., and flew the Lancaster on this visit to Holland. He recalls the Manna fly-past as a really impressive event, though even that was not without its difficulties. "When you have so many aircraft, all with different cruising speeds, trying to keep them together - let alone in loose formation - needed constant attention and concentration."

Lancaster over flat lands. View from astrodome looking towards mid upper turret.

The following day was Holland's national Liberation Day. There were to be three fly-pasts: the first over the Royal Palace; the second over a disused airfield where the Canadians were holding a commemoration for many of their countrymen who died in Holland; and the third over a small village where a street was being re-named in memory of Flight Sergeant Thompson.

(Flight Sergeant Thompson was a Wireless Operator on 9 Squadron. On 1 January 1945, Thompson's aircraft - on a raid on the Dortmund-Ems Canal - was badly hit by a sizeable shell and set on fire. From his position in the centre of the Lancaster, Flight Sergeant Thompson went back and rescued the Mid-upper Gunner; then returned for the Rear Gunner who was unconscious and whose clothes were on fire. Only one of the Gunners survived - he was Dutch and came from the village of Heesch. Flight Sergeant Thompson died three weeks later from his injuries and burns: he was awarded the Victoria Cross.)

During their stay in Holland, the B.B.M.F. aircraft were based at Soesterberg. A request had been received from the British Defence Attache for the sister of Flight Sergeant Thompson, now a very elderly lady, to visit the Flight and be shown over the Lancaster. This had been agreed but there was some confusion over the timing, and her party arrived during the Briefing for the Fly-pasts.

So Squadron Leader Groombridge detailed Sergeant Blackah of the Ground Crew to take her party over to the Lancaster on the other side of the airfield and do the honours. So far so good.

Sergeant Blackah thought it wise, before anyone entered the Lancaster, to get them together and warn them of the hazards and obstructions which they would find in the fuselage. While he was thus briefing them at the foot of the short ladder leading to the entrance hatch, Flight Sergeant Thompson's sister - perhaps she didn't hear, perhaps she was over-eager - started to climb the ladder, lost her balance and fell, gashing her leg badly.

There were emergency calls; the paramedics and an ambulance rushed out, and the elderly lady received immediate treatment. All very unfortunate, though the story did have a happy ending in that, some time later, Flight Sergeant Thompson's sister visited Coningsby and had an incident-free tour of the Lancaster.

But it was not the end of trouble for Sergeant Blackah, or the aircrew. Squadron Leader Groombridge takes up the story: " When we arrived at the Lancaster, we were told that the fuel had not arrived. Of course, very few pure piston-engined aircraft use Soesterberg these days and only a small quantity of Avgas is kept there. What there was had been taken up by the B17 Sally B. Years ago there was a direct pipeline but this had long since been cut off. We made enquiries, and were told not to worry - a bowser had been despatched from Rotterdam and would be with us shortly. We waited.

Our Flight Engineer did his calculations, and said that no way could we do the three fly-pasts on what we had in the tanks. Time was running short.

We made further enquiries. Yes, they had located the bowser: people were turning out in their thousands for Liberation Day, and our fuel was stuck in the traffic miles away...........

Clearly it was not going to arrive before our time for take-off , and we had a difficult decision to make.

We are not in the business of letting people down. The Lancaster completed the fly-past over the Royal Palace, and over the Canadians, but neither do we risk what is a part of our national heritage. With the Engineer muttering that we needed a following wind to see us over the next field, we returned with great regret - and very little fuel - to Soesterberg. I have always been sorry not to have let the village people of Heesch see the Lancaster, but it was just not worth the risk".

———————— ◉ ————————

One of the features of World War II aircraft was the art-work on the nose. Often these were individual, designed and executed by the crews themselves. Bomber aircraft often carried - besides a design - a bomb for each successful sortie, yellow for a night raid; white for daylight. Now in 1997, Lancaster

PA474 carries the markings of J - Johnny of IX Squadron, complete with the nose legends borne by that aircraft. B.B.M.F. have added two markings of their own - poppies - to mark the 1995 fly-pasts over the Mall to celebrate VE day in May, and VJ day in August when the Lancaster dropped a million poppies on the crowds below. Most of us were not privileged to be there: we watched the spectacle on television.

Very few know the amount of preparation that went into those seconds when it had to happen; exactly on time, and in exactly the right place.

Squadron Leader Groombridge again: " The Briefing was simple. We had the time: the poppies had to be on the Mall; not on Horse Guards Parade, or on the lawns behind Buckingham Palace, not even in the trees, but on the Mall. We said this could be done only at really low level - about 250 feet. As a concession, we were allowed to come down to 750 feet, but no lower.

Now we knew about dropping bombs from the Lancaster - that is well-documented, but there were no ballistics figures for dropping poppies. Wind-speeds and direction could affect a heavy object like a bomb: how much more would it affect poppy petals. Just how much we had to find out for ourselves: in other words we had to practice. The Earl Haig Fund were happy to co-operate and we borrowed the Wainfleet Practice Bombing Range.

In fact, the trials went very well. Flight Lieutenant Mike Chatterton flew the Lancaster; I was on the ground with a stopwatch, and we recorded height, speed, wind-speed and drift, and the rate of poppy drop. We were helped in this by the presence of Chris Jeans who was filming for the Discovery TV series. He came along to Wainfleet with his very expensive camera, and the film he took of the trials proved enormously helpful. When it came to the real thing, we had the added advantage of kind weather and managed to get the drop exactly right.

Actually, it was Chris who came nearest to disaster. After the last successful trial run, we loaded the equipment into my car, Chris angled his tripod in and we set off back to Coningsby. We had gone perhaps two or three miles when Chris suddenly shouted, 'S***! I've left my camera behind! There's eighty thousands pounds worth lying on the sands.'

'Well, we can't go back for it now.'

'For God's sake, why not?'

'I'll show you why not,' I said, stopping the car. I looked at my watch and pointed back towards the range. 'It's America's slot now', and four F15's were just beginning their practice bombing runs. 'They use the real thing for weight simulation but they won't explode.'

Eventually we got back to the range target area, and there was the precious camera. And there, about three yards away, was a dummy bomb. Thank God they missed - at least we hit the Mall!"

———————⊙———————

1995 was a busy year. From April through to October, aircraft of B.B.M.F. flew between two hundred and forty and two hundred and fifty displays and fly-pasts. For the VE anniversary there were actually forty four aircraft 'events' over five days from Coningsby, a record of which Squadon Leader Groombridge is justifiably proud.

"And that included an unscheduled event - or should I say one which was shrouded in secrecy at the time. We were to begin by flying the Lancaster, a Spitfire and the Hurricane down to Northolt, and it was important for it was Paul Shenton's first formation job. It was as much a practice flight before we began the actual displays, and the complication at the last minute was an order to take the President of Israel with us in the Lancaster. You see, President Weismann had actually flown and fought in the Battle of Britain, so it was a compliment both ways.

I said it was a complication because Weismann was probably one of the most heavily guarded of all the visiting Heads of State and we had to accommodate his entourage as well. That meant the Dakota joining the formation, and being re-scheduled for it was due to fly to the Isle of Man the following day......And keeping an eye on Paul Shenton in the Hurricane. Of course, we coped."

"Was that your most difficult moment in the five days?"

"Technically, no. Getting B.B.M.F. over the Concert in Hyde Park at precisely the right moment was difficult and getting that spot-on was very satisfying."

———————⊙———————

"Looking back over your years with the Memorial Flight, can you say what has given you the most satisfaction?"

"Apart from doing good displays at the big airshows, I think the real satisfaction has come from showing the Lancaster to the small events, the village fêtes, and little schools in very remote areas. It's their aircraft as well. I remember one very clearly: I should think the entire population had turned out and gathered in the field next to the school. The children were all gathered together and had made big letters on sheets of what looked like cardboard. As we flew over they held these cards up and it spelled out, 'Welcome B.B.M.F.' We were so pleased we turned and gave them a second run, and

everybody waved. Real lump in the throat stuff."

"Other memories?"

"Yes. You know, most of our displays are south of Coningsby, and coming back late afternoon or early evening after a job well done, and we get over the flat lands........say north of Peterborough, and you know that once you've got the thing landed you'll soon be back home with your family, perhaps have a barbeque, have the grandchildren round. And the aircraft goes quiet; the normal chatter and banter of the crew stops. I'm thinking - and I'm sure the crew were - of the guys who did it for real; who went out over those same flat lands, over the Fens and perhaps out over Holland, and whose only reality was a doubt - whether they would be coming back. That's the real point."

Overleaf: 50th Aniversary of VJ day- '...at least we hit the Mall!' Photograph: Crown Copyright/MoD.

PART 2
INTERVIEWS
WITH THE GUIDES

As part of a Reminiscence Project initiated by Lincolnshire County Council in 1995, I was charged with persuading some of the Flight's Guides to talk about their wartime experiences.

Whilst dedicated to bringing about a wider appreciation of the Flight as a living tribute to those aircrew and groundcrew who lost their lives during the Second World War, the Guides are diffident about talking about their own experiences.

Six of the guides took part and unlike the stories in Part 1 of this book, what follows is a collection of thoughts and memories. These conversations, which took place with author Fiona Sampson during the course of just one day, have no particular structure, but, as is often the way with memories, each one seems to lead to the next in a logical way.

Our thanks go to Jim Brown, Peter Bond, Bob Fitzgerald, Doug Handbury, Bill Kane and Sid Marshall.

Mary Powell, 1997

You went and you went and that was the end of it

Bloody minded was just brave. You went and you went and that was the end of it. And if someone got it you said "Bloody bad luck" and if you got it they said "Bloody bad luck".

I wonder if anyone remembers what I remember clearly. What I remember is the guys, the guys who were lost. And the moment I look at the old photos the sorrow I feel. You'd be barracked, sometimes, four crews to a hut. And one day two crews could have gone. The next day two new crews would fill the beds.

But particularly I remember Johnny Pilot. He was from the Isle of Man and he and I joined up together - we were both navigators - went to different Squadrons and he did one trip and was lost.

And the other one was my best friend in civvy street. He was my wife's brother. He was lost just before D Day.

I went through three pilots before I got on Ops. We went to Operational Training Unit (OTU) - the rule was the pilot had to do an extra flight - "second dickies" - before he could go on Ops. We lost them. When we went back to OTU a second time it was bad enough. In the end they got fed up with us - we were a jinx crew. We lost a navigator too.

We were near enough all youngsters together

At OTU we were put in a room with navigators, pilots and bomb aimers. We just walked around the room and nattered and that was how we crewed up. The engineers came in last, at Conversion Unit.

I was trained out in South Africa and coming back on the boat I got to know this navigator. And at Conversion Unit, there he was as an engineer - he'd had the training, you see. So he became our engineer.

We were near enough all youngsters together.

The crew only started to fly together at OTU. There'd be a pilot, a navigator, a bomb aimer, a wireless operator and often only one gunner.

We went back on Ops from Flying School at Wingworth with five Flying Cadets and a Flying Officer. - And then they took the whole team away because they were all flying instructors.

We were just about to leave OTU and the pilot got

sick and we were split up. They sent me off to 214 Squadron all by myself. And when I crewed up we had three Canadians, two New Zealanders and two pommies. It was chatter all the time - you were pommies (British), kiwis and aussies, but I was really left out of it. Then after we'd done about five ops they said "You'll do"!

This is Ops

The first trip was Moldane on 10/11/43. We went over the Alps, there were just four guns in the valley. "If this is ops -" we said. ...The next ten trips night after night were Berlin. Following that we did the Nuremberg, when we lost ninety five, and we carried on to about D Day. We'd finished five more ops and Bomber Harris sent word that all experienced crews had to stand by for daylight runs. We even got the letter through from Dwight Eisenhower: "Be prepared...". but it didn't happen.

Talking about bombing - just a word about the bombing run. The bomb aimer would take over about three minutes before we got to target. You'd release a flare.   That was a ninety-two million candle power flash. Your camera was turning over. The bombs went, and when they'd gone the aeroplane went up about fifty feet - like an elevator. Then it was our job to check that all the bombs had gone. They could remain in the body of the aeroplane. We had a box with sixteen switches one for each bomb station. We'd press down the sixteen switches and if a light came on you knew a bomb was still on board. Then you would lift the hatch and drop the bomb if you were over Germany, or hang onto it till you were over the North Sea.

But what used to happen was, you had -30° to -40° C. Sometimes the release would get frozen up. Then what would happen was you'd press your switch and as you dropped lower it would thaw out and the bomb would be rolling about - you'd hear it. You were supposed to keep the thing and drop it over the North Sea, in a designated area. But if it was loose you might drop it before then. I showed a bloke who'd been in the Navy round the Flight, and he said he'd been waiting to meet the people who dropped those bombs!

There were two things you kept away from - the Army, who were very trigger-happy, and the Navy!

All a great adventure

You have to remember we were only nineteen then. It was all a great adventure.

We went to Rennes 9/6/44. We'd been told it was a piece of cake. We'd been briefed to go in about 18,000. Our skipper thought "Well, we'll go in about 14,000". Of course the Germans hadn't told us that they'd moved all the flak in. They directed it all at us. I remember the rear gunner saying "Good God". On this bombing run our port inner caught fire - but luckily we had fire extinguishers fitted in the engine and put it out. And I managed to drop the bombs - you were supposed to check all the bombs had gone before you started for home. But then we lost the hydraulics - because we lost the starboard inner engine. And then I found I had a bomb hanging in the bomb bay - and having lost our two inner engines and the bomb door being closed, I was unable to release the bomb. The starboard outer was dickey and the oil pressure was low. The Lanc will fly on one inner and not on one outer. But we got back - about one and a half hours late. We'd still got the 500 pounder on board - we had one tyre punctured - we landed and did two groundloops off the runway. ...You have never seen seven chaps get out of a Lanc so quickly! We went straight on leave and when we got back, the ground staff told us there were two hundred shrapnel holes in the plane.

"There's a bloke above us"

We were never held up because of weather on ops. If the weather was a factor, they took that into account. We used two systems of target marking, one with an Australian name and the other a New Zealand. One was Paramata, that was the ground marker. The other was Wanganui, which was used above the clouds - red flares. The reason their names were Aussie and New Zealander was that the chief of Pathfinders was Air Vice Marshall A V Bennett - an Australian.

At first bombing was very approximate. You were lucky if you were within miles of the target. And if a Pathfinder was hit, it would crash maybe ten miles from target and its target indicators would burst on impact, then everyone would bomb that. Even over the target we had to be careful when we dropped our bombs. There'd be aircraft below us - at five hundred feet. The Halifax went only to about 20,000 feet. The mid upper gunner would say "There's a bloke above us" - so you'd be judging all the time. One aircraft flew all the way back from an op with a delayed action bomb lodged in one of his engine shells. He flew all the way back to our base, was instructed to put the aircraft out to sea, set the automatic pilot and ditched. The aircraft flew back across the North Sea and finally crashed in Holland. And after the war we heard that the Germans had found this aircraft and had spent several days searching for the crew. They thought the local people were hiding the crew; of course they never found anybody!

I was the rear gunner. It's like being in a capsule in space. I think the Browning ·303 was a good machine gun because you'd got 22ft of solid bullets. The ·5 goes a bit further, but is slow. A ·303 will down an assault plane as easy as a ·5. It fires 1,200 rounds a minute.

Means of escape and survival

Aircrew were very thoroughly briefed on means of escape and survival when they were shot down. When you were going out on ops you weren't allowed to take anything with you at all other than your dog tag - that's your identity. When you went into briefing, you'd go into this briefing room which was just an ordinary room with a big map on the wall. And you were ticked off by the police and unless your name was on the list you didn't go in. When everyone was in and the door was locked there would be a big map on the wall and the route was marked with red ribbon.

You were briefed by senior officers. Each category of crew had a leader and each in turn would brief their people as to what their part would be in the operation. Finally the Group Captain would give you his bullshit talk: the importance of each chap etc.

We'd hand round bags. In that would be an escape kit, which contained all sorts of things: chocolate, two packets of English chewing gum, a postcard, barley sugars, a fish hook - you'd also get some currency. All of this was carried for if you got shot down and managed to bail out. You were told it was your duty to escape.

You'd to empty your pockets. You put all your stuff in your bags that you took the escape kit from - you got it back when you came back - or if you didn't come back it was sent to your next of kin.

Later in the war they had escape boots. Our boots were lace-up but had a fur top to them. If you were trying to escape you were supplied with a knife to cut the fur. The old boots were a give away. But we needed the fur. We gunners had to have ankle socks so that our boots didn't come off. We had electric suits, heavy kopak suits.

We kept going...

We kept going with "Wakey-wakey" tablets - they were caffeine - and we had barley sugars. We had chocolate which was too hard to break and orange juice, in cans, which was frozen at -40° C. Our mechanic used to love it when we chucked him a can of orange juice for his kids. We had bacon and eggs on take-off and landing: that was something civvies didn't have. The other thing we used to get was sheets on the bed and pillowcases. Ordinary ranks didn't.

And when we came back we went into debriefing and all the crew would sit round a table, with an intelligence officer taking notes about what we'd seen. On the table there were five trays of fags and you filled your pockets with these and no matter what time of day it was you could cut the air; it was blue! And you also had a rum ration and you could have it in your cocoa or neat. I couldn't stand rum so our mid-upper gunner always had my tot.

"It does seem a bit daft"

It does seem a bit daft to camouflage planes when there's a great circle like a target painted on them!

There was an electric muff on the cannons in the rear turret to stop them freezing, and one night I got so bloody cold I took it off and put it on my head. Luckily we weren't being attacked...!

The Lanc had 2,154 gallons of petrol, fully loaded: three tanks in each wing. The only time we carried that much was when we went to Köningsberg. At the briefing the engineers were saying to us "For God's sake be careful with the petrol!". We used to get up early and ask the lads what bomb load and what fuel they were putting in. You'd have a rough idea of where you were going before you went into briefing. The Lancaster did about one mile to the gallon and that made it easy to work out.

The first Frieburg raid we were flying between two banks of cloud. There was St Elmo's Fire all round the plane. We tried to climb up over the second bank of cloud to escape it but we couldn't. It was very bumpy!

The night we went to Munich; that's ten hours of flying - and in a turret that's no joke. On the way we went through lots of searchlights. When we got to Munich it was a hotbed of flak. But it had been marked for us at 1,000 feet by a Master Bomber in a Mosquito. How he managed at that height! But he came back and got a VC the next day - not for that, for some other op. We lost an engine to the flak. When we got back over the UK the skipper said "I think we'll stop at Gerrards Cross. It's an American base; we'll get plenty to eat". Well we just managed to land on three engines. When we got down the engines cut out - even before we could taxi in. Well, we got picked up in a jeep and taken to the mess. There were dustbins overflowing with food all the way down and as we got to the counter the man pulled down the grill and said "Sorry mate, you've missed it"!

Taking a chance on life

For good luck, I used to whistle "Taking a Chance on Love". I called it "Taking a Chance on Life". The tune in '42-'43 was "Deep in the Heart of Texas". Air crew generally were very superstitious. Everyone took something up with them. We took WAAF stockings. Our rear gunner had a long rainbow scarf he'd wrap around his neck: wouldn't fly without it. We wouldn't allow photography of any kind on the station - because it was a jinx. Well, two of our chaps completed 100 trips. Out

came these reporters from the Daily Sketch, I think it was. They took lots of photos; and on the next trip they were shot down.

In '42 we didn't have H2S, we had Fishpond: that was an anti-flak. And Monica: the rear gunner had that. We had G, but that only went a certain way into Europe. Later we had Lorraine - long range G.*

Soon as the war was over we went on a circular tour of the Rhür to take photos. Seventeen of us flew out in a Lanc for a naughty weekend in Berlin for the chaps with the most trips. Everything was smashed to the ground. Absolutely kaput and the smell of death was unbearable. The Reichstag knocked to pieces. And the biggest dandelion I've ever seen waving over a small crater. We took bishops, judges, people like that on a Cooks Tour of Berlin. We were followed everywhere by a crowd of Germans. They were living in the sewers.

You could have bought half of Berlin for a quarter pound of coffee.

We were in Cairo. The kids there were little devils. Two or three mates were ahead of me and I was walking along in uniform. It was the time when they kept making Cairo in and out of bounds. Suddenly all these kids descended on me - "Captain! Captain!" - and of course they picked my pocket.

Wartime Lancaster dropping sticks of incendiaries.

(Photograph: Crown Copyright/MoD)

Calais

We did a raid to Calais - it was bad weather - we went in really low - 500 ft - we couldn't get through. A little later we were told to go out again to take photos of the target. We were really rushed. It's hard to get back to check for a camera flash - it's in the tail end in a Wellington - so I asked the WOP (Wireless Operator) "Is there a camera flash on board?" - "Yes I think so". I went back and checked and there wasn't. And I said to the skipper "You must stop, there's no point in going, we haven't got a camera flash", the skipper said "Well don't worry, I'll take the rap". But when we came back I got a severe reprimand and my promotion was put back six months.

*Explanatory Footnotes:

Fishpond: A device that located aircraft coming up from behind and below. They were picked up from the H2S scanner: an indicator was located on the right hand side of the Wireless Operator's table.

Monica: A device which picked up the radar from the enemy's night-fighter scanner which was trying to track you. Short range.

Gee: A navigation aid. Picked up radio signals from Home stations in triangular formation.

Lorraine: Long distance Gee.

H2S: Another navigation aid. Airborne radar transmitter/receiver.

About the Author

Peter Rowland served in the RAF from 1944-48 (trained as a pilot) and on the Reserve until 1954. He held a Private Pilots' Licence until 1990 when he could no longer fudge his way through the medical.

He has been a Volunteer Guide with the Flight since November 1986.

BATTLE OF BRITAIN
MEMORIAL FLIGHT
VISITOR CENTRE

RAF Coningsby, Lincolnshire, LN4 4SY
Tel: 01526 344041

This irreplaceable collection - 2 Hurricanes, 5 Spitfires, a Dakota and the only Lancaster still flying in Europe - is maintained as a living tribute to the RAF aircrew and groundcrew who gave their lives in World War II.

Open Monday to Friday 10am to 5pm. Last tour starts 3.30pm.
Closed Easter, Bank Holidays and two weeks at Christmas.
Admission charged.

If you are making a special journey it is advisable to telephone first to check the availability of aircraft, especially between May and September.

Lancaster PA474 displaying its markings of J - Johnny of IX Squadron. BBMF have added two poppies to mark the 1995 flypasts over the Mall to celebrate VE day and VJ day(see page 64) shown clearly in this photograph courtesy of Sgt Keith Brenchley.